Changing Times
SERIES

THORNTON CLEVELEYS
remembered

From left to right: Ralph Smedley, Betty Whitaker, Fred Anyon at the 200th anniversary of the first publicity of Cleveleys (see p. 43). The late Betty Whitaker was secretary of the Thornton Cleveleys Chamber of Commerce and Trade, and organized the anniversary dinner. Fred Anyon was guest speaker.

The Prince of Wales meets the council, 1923.

Changing Times
SERIES

THORNTON CLEVELEYS
remembered

Compiled by
Ralph Smedley

TEMPUS

First published 2001
Copyright © Ralph Smedley, 2001

Tempus Publishing Limited
The Mill, Brimscombe Port,
Stroud, Gloucestershire, GL5 2QG

ISBN 0 7524 2277 4

Typesetting and origination by
Tempus Publishing Limited
Printed in Great Britain by
Midway Colour Print, Wiltshire

Cleveleys beach, opposite Victoria Road, *c*. 1928. A young Fred Ayon can be seen on the right in shorts and a Baines blazer; the Jolly Tars are in the background.

Contents

Acknowledgements

I would like to thank Enid Lewis for assistance with typing and preparation of the manuscript for publication, Tony Gaynor for writing an introduction, Ted Lightbown for the loan of photographs and the *Blackpool Evening Gazette* for access to their old copies of the *Gazette & Herald* and the *Thornton Cleveleys Times*. Special thanks go to my wife Ann for her encouragement and support throughout the book's preparation.

The bathing platform at Rossall Beach, Thornton Cleveleys, in the late 1920s.

Introduction

Journalist Fred Anyon spent his whole working life with the local newspaper, the *Gazette &
Herald* (later the *Thornton Cleveleys Times*) and over the many years at his desk wrote regular
local interest pieces that were read and enjoyed by a generation of readers. Fred was a fount of
knowledge on the area and was always pleased to give help and advice on matters of local
interest and local history. This book is a kind of tribute to his writing on local matters and
consists of a selection of extracts written over several decades, beginning in the 1940s and
extending to the 1980s. Most of the pieces here are attributable to him. Accompanying the
extracts is a remarkable selection of contemporary photographs and other illustrations that
bring to life these fascinating articles about Thornton Cleveleys. Many who knew Fred well will
recall his favourite quip: 'Just nipped home for some lunch – pheasant and chips!'
    Fred Anyon died in 1995 and this tribute appeared in the *Blackpool Evening Gazette*:

Former Editor Dies Aged Eighty

A well-loved character of Cleveleys, retired journalist Fred Anyon, has died. The former editor
of the *Thornton Cleveleys Times*, Mr Anyon, who was eighty, was an accomplished after-dinner
speaker.
The former Baines Grammar School pupil, who died yesterday, entered journalism as a cuts
reporter on the staff of the *Fleetwood Chronicle* in 1933. After serving in the Army during the
war he returned to journalism in 1949 to the *Gazette*'s Cleveleys office to work as a reporter.
The bachelor, who was known to many friends as Bob, later became editor of the *Thornton
Cleveleys Times*.
Mr Anyon, of Clarence Avenue, Cleveleys, also worked at the *Gazette*'s St Annes and
Blackpool editorial departments.
Betty Whittaker, secretary of the Cleveleys Chamber of Commerce, paid tribute to the veteran
journalist. She said: 'He was one of the great characters, he really was one of the stalwarts of
Cleveleys. He was a lovely man. He will be greatly missed.'

Blackpool Evening Gazette, 22 April 1995

Victoria Road, Thornton Cleveleys.

Roy Castle (right) around 1947-1948 on a Gala Float advertising 'Happiness Ahead'.

Thornton Cleveleys: The Early Days

The coast of Lancashire from the River Mersey northwards to Morecambe Bay would, for centuries, have consisted mainly of sand dunes, together with sandstone cliffs and pebbly beaches towards the northerly end in the Fylde coast area of the county. An area such as this, exposed to westerly winds for most of the year, was far too hostile a climate for most people to live and as a consequence was sparsely populated. Such hamlets as there were, were generally some miles inland.

Seaside places, such as Blackpool, didn't come to the notice of the world at large until the establishment of a daily coach service to Blackpool in 1783. There was at that time an 'explosion' of interest in sea bathing at Brighton, Scarborough and other resorts mainly in the south. Blackpool consisted of a few hotels and about fifty thatched dwellings spread along the coast. Visitors at that time were confined to cotton-mill owners and professional people. This remained the case until the coming of the railway to the Fylde in 1840 and to Blackpool in 1846. The advent of the railway meant that holidays by the sea became the accepted arrangement for the working classes of Lancashire, the employees of the mill owners.

Typical of the professional people coming to Blackpool was Dr John Cocker, who arrived about 1830 from Blackburn. He came in bad health but more especially because he was driven out of Blackburn by a gambling debt. Cocker erected the Victoria Promenade, later known as the Crystal Palace, in the town centre. He and his family lived at Eringo Lodge, set amongst the sand dunes about three miles to the north of the town.

The 1860s saw the development of the Claremont Park estate northwards from Blackpool's North pier towards the Gynn and with it the building of hotels to provide more amenable accommodation for those of independent means. Another reason why the development was situated here was because it was distant from the boarding house accommodation for the working classes around the railway stations.

This trend for the building of hotels and other amenities along the coast, both northwards and southwards, was to carry on until the 1940s, a trend that was to result in separate townships emerging in the form of St Annes to the south and Bispham and Cleveleys to the north. Following the popularity of sea bathing for all, came the fashion for hydropathic treatment at the bigger hotels. Typical amongst these was the Imperial Hotel on Blackpool's North Shore, the Norbreck Hydro north of Bispham and the Cleveleys Hydro further north still. The word 'hydro', of course, is an abbreviation of 'hydropathic', which simply meant specialized baths of brine with associated treatments. Over and above this there were recreations such as golf, tennis and croquet, and conservatories where one could relax and converse with fellow patrons of a similar social class.

No doubt a similar ambience existed at the hotels away from Blackpool to the south at Lytham St Annes, where there were as many as four eighteen-hole golf courses.

Many would say that the principal industry of Cleveleys for most of the twentieth century was catering for the needs of the holidaymaker by providing accommodation from the grandiose level of the Hydro down to the humble bed and breakfast away from the sea front. Thornton (Cleveleys' older brother town), two miles inland from the sea, had industry of a more traditional kind, in the shape of the chemical industry. This from 1926 was known as ICI, but it had origins more than fifty years earlier in the form of a salt works, which came about almost by accident.

In the 1850s haematite, a rich form of iron ore, was found at Barrow. This proved a very lucrative find and was the basis on which Barrow's shipbuilding industry and future prosperity were to depend. It was considered that if the ore was sited on the north side of Morecambe Bay then there was a distinct possibility of similar deposits on the south side of the bay, perhaps in the area around the mouth of the River Wyre.

Drilling in the Preesall area, east of the Wyre, failed to locate any iron ore deposits, but unlimited amounts of rock salt were found below the surface. If iron ore was to be the source of

Barrow's prosperity, then similarly the salt workings of Preesall were to be the raw material of comparable riches in terms of employment in Thornton and the surrounding area for more than 120 years.

The United Alkali Company opened its works alongside the railway line and close to the River Wyre at the north end of Thornton in an area known as Burn Naze. Its location by the river enabled coasters to off-load limestone shipped from North Wales. The finished product was shipped out by rail wagons.

Up to the Second World War the chemical manufacture was confined to the production of washing soda used in the production of glass. It was also used in the cotton industry as well as in its better-known uses around the home. The green fields south of the 'Chemic', as it was known locally, stretched all the way to Thornton station and along the River Wyre as far as Skippool. All came to an abrupt halt with the necessary demands for war-orientated chemicals based on chlorine, which was also derived from Preesall salt. On those green fields were built chemical factories far greater in extent than the old works.

At least a dozen men played a part in the development of Thornton Cleveleys in the first two decades of the twentieth century, but one in particular stands out: T.G. Lumb. He came from Manchester where he had qualified as an architect. After service with the Lancashire and Yorkshire Railway, he joined a firm of civil engineers in Preston and in 1892 became the manager of their Blackpool office. He was to spend the rest of his life on the Fylde coast.

He prepared plans and supervised construction of the Blackpool to Fleetwood tramway, which opened in 1898; at that time he was still in his thirties. His vision, which he frequently described in his lifetime, was a City of the Fylde stretching from Lytham to Fleetwood. He believed that there was an enormous future awaiting the area if only it could be developed. At that time most of the coastal strip consisted of sand dunes. There were only a handful of houses and farms at Cleveleys. Between Cleveleys and Rossall School there was only College Farm.

In 1900, when still only thirty-eight years old, he started in business on his own and was invited to join a syndicate of businessmen to purchase 1,000 acres known as the Fleetwood Estates from Thornton Gate to Fleetwood. In 1904 the Fleetwood Estate Company bought the Thornton Estate from the Horrocks Estates, which with the above 1,000 acres made a total of more than 2,000 acres. This huge tract of land was ripe for development and a start was made at Rossall Beach, immediately south of Rossall School, and at Thornton Gate, an area about three-quarters of a mile north of Cleveleys tram station.

Helping Tom Lumb with this project was a young architect, Mr E.L. Lutyens, who designed several houses in the Rossall Beach area. Later Lutyens was to design the Menin Gate at Ypres and the Viceroy's palace in Delhi.

Cleveleys, like the rest of the Fylde coast, and for that matter the whole of the old Lancashire coast, is what sailors in previous centuries, and no doubt modern yachtsmen, would call a lee-shore, in that the prevailing westerly wind is likely to drive a sailing ship onto it. This has probably been a problem in bad weather as long as ships have plied the Irish Sea.

The development of Liverpool as a port in the seventeenth and eighteenth centuries, with a large number of sailing vessels entering and leaving the port, must have produced many shipwrecks along the Fylde Coast. The following is a list of the more outstanding shipwrecks of the last 150 years:

Crusader (1840), after which the sandbank of that name off the shore at Lytham St Annes is called.

Mexico (1886), in the Ribble estuary, which accounted for the loss of the lifeboat crews of both St Annes and Southport lifeboats in the rescue of the crew of the sailing ship by the Lytham lifeboat.

Syrene and *Foudroyant* (1897), both very near to Blackpool North Pier.

Abana (1895) further north at Bispham.

The *Abana* is particularly interesting because the skeleton of the wooden remains are still visible between Little Bispham and Anchorsholme, to the south of Cleveleys. More than a hundred years later the wooden bones of the *Abana*, having been washed by the tide almost 80,000 times, remain as a testimony to a gallant rescue.

It may well be thought that the lifeboat *Samuel Fletcher* is long since gone. Not so: it can be seen plying much calmer waters as a pleasure launch on Blackpool's Stanley Park lake, more than 100 years after the *Abana* and other heroic rescues of sailing-ship days.

The most prestigious hotel in Cleveleys by far was the Hydro, situated about half a mile south of where Victoria Road meets the Promenade. It was originally a private house called Eringo Lodge, the home of a Dr J. Cocker who came to the Fylde about 1830. He may be called one of the 'founding fathers' of Blackpool. Both he and his son figured largely in the establishment of the town and the son became the first mayor of the borough in 1876. Incidentally the name 'Eringo' is from the botanical name for the sea holly, *Ibex eringo*, which even in the heyday of the Hydro thrived happily amongst the sand dunes which were once a feature of the coast from north of the cliffs at Norbreck all the way to Fleetwood.

Cleveleys has always been in the shadow of Blackpool and could therefore never expect to have live entertainment to match such a major seaside resort. However, from the 1920s to the 1950s, Cleveleys had, surprisingly enough, theatrical shows at two venues during the season.

Firstly, there was the Arena by the road junction at the top of Victoria Road, where the open-air theatre was situated beneath the Promenade, facing inland. The show there was what was known at that time as The Follies and was a succession of variety acts. It would be like many shows at the smaller seaside resorts around the country during the summer season and consisted of singers, dancing girls and musical instruments. Admission was charged somewhat casually: the seated audience paid for the use of deck chairs, whereas a collecting box went round those standing at the back. The show was in the capable hands of Charlie Parsons, who was the link man and resident comedian.

The other theatrical venue was 400 yards further south along the Promenade at the Queens Theatre. The essential difference between the two venues was that while the Arena specialized mainly in afternoon entertainment, the Queens hosted almost exclusively evening shows, for which the paying audience had comfortable seats.

In addition to the two theatres there were four cinemas in Thornton Cleveleys, three in Cleveleys and one in Thornton. The three in Cleveleys were the Odeon, the Savoy and the Pavilion. From an architectural standpoint the Odeon was supreme, being of an Art Deco design. It was opened in 1935. The Savoy was a middle-of-the-range cinema and was in Victoria Road, nearer the Promenade than most of the shops. The films featured there were not as recently released as those at the Odeon. The Pavilion was an asbestos-clad building and again stood in Victoria Road. The films were of the older variety, such as *Old Mother Riley* and *Abbott and Costello*. The fare on offer was a reflection of the fact that the audience were towards the younger end of the cinema-going public.

The cinema in Thornton was the Verona and was situated near to the Gardeners Arms Hotel on Fleetwood Road. The audience would be the residents of Thornton and few visitors would be numbered amongst them.

Tony Gaynor, 2001

Bourne Hall, *c.* 1912.

A Battlefield 1,000 Years Old

Ancient Bourne Hall, Thornton's most historic home, has new tenants this month, adding another name to the renowned list of families who have lived at the hall which, for centuries, has stood like a sentinel between the Wyre and the sea.

Messrs R.W. Edmondson and Son of Fleetwood succeed the Cowell family who farmed Bourne Hall for at least fifty years. The hall passed from the Cowell family following the death of Mr William Cowell earlier in the year.

There is not a lot of recorded history about Thornton. This is a pity because we should like to know more about places like Bourne Hall, which, by the way, was called Burn Hall when I was a lad.

It is known that there has been a house on the hill for 800 years or more and that the present building was erected by the Westbys of Mowbreck Hall in the sixteenth century. Eventually the Fleetwoods acquired it and finally it became one of the dozen or so farms belonging to the Fleetwood Estate Company – a number that has dwindled to seven with the development of the district.

Included in Thornton Cleveleys Council's recently published book of local scenes is a picture of a ceiling at the hall, ornamented with vine leaves and clusters of grapes. This was all that remained of the finery of a domestic chapel that had oak panelling, carved shields and statues and was demolished to preserve the cheese-room, into which the apartment had been converted, from infestation by rats. Over the entrance to this room was a Latin inscription of the verse from the Psalms which begins, 'I had rather be a doorkeeper' – the same text that they put on the tablet in Thornton parish church to the memory of that grand old schoolmaster, Mr George Hardman, who served so long as warden and sidesman.

There has always been a story about a very big battle that lasted from sunrise to sunset on the hill. Local historians have hunted for information about it and still remain unsatisfied. It is supposed to have been fought 1,000 years ago, when the Danes made a vigorous attempt to regain Northumbria. That there was a famous battle at this time is not in doubt, and there is an ancient poem about it. The point at issue is whether the site mentioned is Bourne Hill. If so, then Thornton is a sort of northern Hastings – only on this occasion our side won!

The only bit of history I remember coming out of the hill was when Mr Jack Rawcliffe, who used to drive our steam roller, *Victoria*, found a dagger 18 inches long. He was using the roller for pulling up trees and hedges when the council was straightening the road. The dagger tumbled out of some loose soil. The last time I saw it, it was reposing on a shelf in the pumping station, a rusty reminder that there may be lots of museum pieces under the turf of Bourne Hill.

In the eighteenth century, one Thomas Tyldesley of Foxhall, a friend of the Westbys, lived nearby. An entry in his diary for June 1715 reads: 'Went to Mains to prayers; thence with Jack Westby to Burn for dinner, stayed till 4; thence to Whinneyheys, stayed till 9, soe home.' Can't you imagine the two horsemen coming over the marshlands of Thornton, in sight of cottages that are still standing and the view they must have had from the hall – no factories, no Fleetwood, only the green plain of the deserted peninsula?

Going back earlier, to the persecution of Roman Catholics, it may be that among those who have hidden in Bourne Hall was Father Campion, the celebrated Jesuit, for when he was caught and tortured he mentioned John Westby as one who had helped him in Lancashire.

Before he was taken out to the Tower and executed, Campion declared in a letter his sorrow at having confessed: 'It grieved me much to have offended the Catholic cause so highly, as to confess the names of some gentlemen and friends in whose houses I have been entertained; yet in this I greatly cherish and comfort myself, that I never disclosed any secrets there declared and that I will not, come rack, come rope.'

What a lot of glamour Bourne Hall has lost as it has become less isolated! First came industry on the eastern landscape, and now it has reached the foot of the hill and the old winding lane is but a memory. You need a lot of imagination to picture it in its former romantic setting. It is best to approach on a dark night, with a ghostly wind rustling through the orchard and eerie cries of seabirds from the marsh, to feel something of the grandeur that has gone.

The last time I was at the farm they were selling the fine herd of Friesian cattle. If there were any ghosts of knights and squires, priests-in-hiding or headless horsemen about, I didn't see them. I must call again when the moon is out.

Once there was a teacher at Thornton who lived at Bourne Hall, and long before I had seen it I heard about its long dark corridors, its concealed staircases and hiding places. It was much lonelier then and she admitted being a bit scared going to the hall on winter nights, with so many stories of the spirits of the departed and such things that are easy to think about when trees cast shadows, and owls are hooting. But all that belongs to the past and now Bourne Hall stands like a sturdy old retainer scanning the ever-changing carucates of the Domesday survey and awaiting further encroachments upon the green slopes – one of which, the council has ordained, shall be a cemetery.

1 June 1946

Moving the Big Dipper to London

The mythical bird, the phoenix, was endowed with unusual properties; when cremated it arose from the ashes as fit and as frisky as ever. This week a familiar landmark in Cleveleys, the scenic railway at the Pleasure Beach off North Promenade, has disappeared but, like the phoenix, it's due for another lease of life – 280 miles away.

This little 'Big Dipper' is going to London, where a new, glittering and glamorous life awaits it at Battersea Park Fun Fair, now nearing completion for the opening of the Festival of Britain in May.

The 40ft high 'figure of eight' switch-back railway has recently been bought by Messrs John Collins, the largest firm of fairground contractors in the country and principal contractors for the much-publicized Battersea Fun Fair. The reason for their purchase of the Cleveleys scenic railway was the chronic shortage of timber, so serious that it is worth their while dismantling it, transporting it by rail to London and re-erecting it there.

Fifteen men started dismantling operations here last week and are hoping to finish the job this weekend. Nearly half a dozen loads of timber have been sent daily to Thornton goods station at Hillylaid where, every day, several loaded wagons are being sent to Poulton. There, a special train of between fifty and sixty wagons is being assembled by British Railways and the Cleveleys 'Big Dipper' – about 200 tons of it altogether – will soon start its long journey to Battersea and, it is hoped, will help to earn dollars and other coveted foreign currencies.

Thornton stationmaster, Mr W.H. Iddon, has been spending a good deal of his time at the goods station this week. 'Of its kind, this is probably the biggest job we've ever tackled here,' he says. Mr Iddon is doubtful whether one train will be sufficient to transport 200 tons of timber. 'It's not so much the weight that matters, but the bulk,' he said this week while seeing timber being manhandled from wagons onto 45ft Bogie Bolsters with a carrying capacity of 40 tons. Every load has to be carefully roped and chained to comply with safety regulations.

The railway staff at Thornton had only one week's notice of this big move and special wagons have had to be brought to Thornton from all parts of the north of England. There was a tense moment early this week when Stationmaster Iddon and Inspector Johnson of Warrington were

Jubilee Walk, Cleveleys.

The Big Dipper, Cleveleys.

discussing the move.

With masses of timber piled high on the wagons, Inspector Johnson, who is in charge of goods for this region, doubted whether the wagons would pass under the nearby railway gauge. Stationmaster Iddon thought they might, but he was far from sure. When a test was made, the wagons passed under the gauge with about three inches to spare, and forty or fifty workmen and railway employees at the goods station heaved a sigh of relief.

If present arrangements are carried out without any serious hitches, dismantling operations at the Fairground will be completed today and by Monday or Tuesday the special train at Poulton sidings should be ready to leave for London.

This is the kind of job that could not possibly be undertaken by road haulage firms; it's a job for the railway. The cost of the move plus the cost of re-erecting the scenic railway at Battersea is likely to be in the region of £2,000 and Messrs John Collins already have an 'outsize' scenic railway nearing completion at Battersea Park; the Cleveleys railway will be additional to this.

This week Cleveleys Pleasure Beach, most of which was occupied by the 'Big Dipper', looks uncannily like one of the Ruhr cities after a war-time 'saturation' raid by Allied air forces. Huge mounds of rubble, rain-soaked planks and rusting piles of debris give a very forlorn appearance to the scene; probably a fairground always looks rather doleful and depressing in mid-winter.

On Tuesday, when I was there, underneath one of the yet-to-be dismantled pillars was a man busily occupied with a circular saw cutting up some of the surplus timber for sale. When asked whether there was a ready sale for this firewood at three shillings a bag he replied, 'They take it faster than I can cut it.' Was any stolen by unauthorized nocturnal visitors? 'Yes, a good deal,' he admitted ruefully, 'and they'll have to think of a better excuse than the fuel shortage if I catch them!'

27 January 1951

15

The 'Happy Ever After' Wreck

A shipwreck is usually a horrendous event. The very word conjures up visions of broken spars and drowned men, another defeat in a relentless battle against the elements.

The great wind of December 1894 produced a small miracle by depositing on the sands of a seaside resort what was to become a source of wonder and excitement to generations of children; and all this without a great deal of fuss, or any injuries at all.

Blackpool was preening its feathers in the hope of becoming a major holiday resort. The Tower had recently been completed, and hopes were high. The outlying areas had scarcely been touched at all; Bispham, Norbreck and Cleveleys were mainly rural communities sandwiched between the brash new glamour of Blackpool and the burgeoning new town and port of Fleetwood. It was on their hitherto undiscovered beaches that the prize was about to be delivered.

The date was 22 December 1894, three days before Christmas. The barque *Abana* was under comparatively new ownership, having spent the first twenty years of her life carrying timber from Canada to Britain under the Canadian flag. She was built in Portland, New Brunswick, and registered originally at St John. She was a fair size for her day – 1,269 tons net; now she was registered at Farsund, Norway.

A few months earlier she had been sold to Norwegian owners and was currently bound for Florida in ballast. She had sailed from Liverpool days before, but bad weather had forced her to shelter off the Isle of Man.

Then, all hell broke loose. What turned out to be one of the worst hurricanes ever to hit these shores roared in across the Irish Sea. So strong were the winds that there were fears for the brand-new Tower. Probably many people were quaking in their boots about their investment; so much so that two officials mounted the structure in the very teeth of the hurricane, the paper says.

All was well; not so at sea. Let the reporter from the local newspaper take up the story, in an account published some days later.

'The hurricane blew with unabated violence until late Saturday afternoon, and a constant look-out was kept from both North and Central piers for any vessel that might be in distress. About three o'clock the lookout on the North Pier sighted a large ship in the offing, drifting in a north-westerly direction. She was a three-masted barque, with all her sails torn to ribbons and was evidently unmanageable.

On she came, as helpless as a log upon the ocean, and at length, shortly after five o'clock, she grounded close to the cliffs about half a mile beyond Norbreck. Meanwhile, the vessel had been observed at Bispham, and a crowd gathered on the cliffs to watch its progress. The barque came ashore bow first, but was soon slewed broadside on by the force of the waves.

Signals of distress were fired from the vessel and these were quickly answered by those on shore, who lit a fire on the face of the cliff and fed it with a tar barrel and whatever fuel they could lay their hands on. A boy was despatched with all speed to Blackpool to summon the lifeboat crew, but the signals had in the meantime been noticed at North Pier, from which word was quickly passed to the lifeboat men that their services were required.

Coxswain Cartmell had his men in readiness, and the boat was soon despatched on her errand of mercy. The journey was a long and tedious one, the boat having to be taken by road on a detour of seven miles via Bispham. It was thus eight o'clock when the *Samuel Fletcher* and her brave crew reached the scene of the wreck, and the boat was launched some distance to the North of Little Bispham slade. The wreck lay inside the Shell Wharf, and about 150 yards from the shore. By the time the lifeboat was launched it was high water and the sea was breaking over the deck of the barque.

The lifeboat was well manned, there being sixteen crew, and the oars were double-banked. It was rather awkward for the boat to reach the vessel, on account of the terrible surf that was running at the time, but the coxswain steered her nicely to the lee side of the wreck and was

The Wreck of the *Abana*, port and starboard side, December 1894.

soon alongside. It was perilous work, however, for the yards of the mainmast hung over the side of the vessel and there was some danger of its giving way and falling on the brave band of rescuers.

"How many can you take?" shouted the captain of the shipwrecked mariners immediately the lifeboat got within hailing distance. "There are seventeen of us!" he added. "We can take you all!" was the coxswain's cheery reply, and the men tumbled into the lifeboat until all were saved with a celerity that showed how exceedingly glad they were to quit their unfortunate vessel.

The lifeboat was then turned to the nearest point shorewards, but with thirty-three men on board the *Samuel Fletcher* was rather deep in the water, and the keel stuck on top of the sandbank. Some of the boatmen, however, leaped into the water, pushed her afloat, then sprang back into her, and the channel was crossed safely.

Rescued and rescuers had a hearty welcome when they landed. Mrs Hardman was particularly kind in seeing to their welfare. They were taken to the Red Lion Hotel, where hot coffee and rum, milk, tea and every refreshment the men could wish was served to them. It was indeed an impressive sight as the thirty-three men walked into the hotel clad in cork lifebelts and oilskins, and looking thoroughly drenched. After partaking of Mrs Hardman's hospitality, and the horses having been attended to, the lifeboat men set out homeward, the villagers, headed by the Rector, cheering them to the echo.'

So the lifeboatmen were safely on their way, doubtless flowing with good ale and the satisfaction of a job well done. Many of them were young men who had never been out before, which makes the rescue all the more remarkable. I dare say even the horses who had dragged the boat so far felt a sense of achievement.

Meanwhile, back at the Red Lion, Capt. Danielsen and his crew of thirteen Norwegian and three Swedish seamen continued to bask in the attentions of the good ladies of the village. There seems to be something about a shipwrecked sailor that appeals to the basic emotions of everyone – particularly the ladies. Besides, our reporter puts it, 'they were all finely built fellows.' He continued with his report:

'Every attention was paid to the shipwrecked seamen, Mrs Castle, the landlord's wife, doing everything in her power to make them comfortable. Large fires were lighted in several rooms, blankets were aired, and in a very short space of time fourteen of the men were cosily ensconced in bed. Two of the others, and a Mr Niblett, of Norbreck, returned at low water and remained there until daybreak, packing the men's effects, and a cartload of boxes was removed to the Hotel, where Mrs Castle, with one or two willing assistants, stayed up all night drying the damp clothing that had been brought in.'

The report goes on: 'Shortly after midnight on Saturday, a mysterious-looking conveyance drove up to the wreck at low water, and when morning broke the sides of the vessel were found to be plastered with the legend, so familiar in Blackpool, "Beecham's Pills"!'

So the advertising world had got into the act too. Beecham's must have had some right go-getters in those days; advertising was, of course, nowhere near the industry it is today. Perhaps it was a little ludicrous, or even downright bad taste, to plaster advertisements on a shipwreck; but that was the brashness of the age. I'm sure they wouldn't have done it had there been any lives lost.

Our intrepid reporter then went on to see the wreck for himself. 'From the hotel our representative journeyed seawards and soon saw the masts and spars of the barque towering above the cliffs. Their appearance bore eloquent, though silent, testimony to the violence of the gale. With the exception of the mainsail, the greater portion of which was reefed, all the canvas had been blown to shreds, and only small and tattered portions were suspended from the yards. The ship's toe-plate had broken off, and lay fifty yards away to the east. The bow lay towards the north, and the vessel had listed to starboard to such an extent that its deck was at an angle of 45 degrees. It was a comparatively easy task, therefore, for our representative to climb up the side of the vessel and reach the deck. It was more difficult for one to retain one's feet on the sloping and slippery floor after descending the companionway, and the peculiar

The crew of the *Abana* on deck shortly before the shipwreck.

sensation made one at first feel quite dizzy. Most of the men were busy packing up, but one stalwart and pleasant-faced young fellow – a Swede, who spoke English very well – managed to spare a few moments to tell his plain unvarnished tale to the adventurous reporter.

"After leaving Liverpool on December fifth," he said, "we experienced very heavy weather, and ran into Ramsey Bay, where we dropped anchor and waited for fairer winds. We lay there until Thursday morning, when the weather became very favourable, and we resumed our course. We had only been out about two hours when the wind turned round, and began to blow fresh from WNW. We took in sails, leaving just sufficient canvas to enable us to steer her, and on Friday morning we passed Holyhead and were in St George's Channel. Owing to the stormy head-wind, we had to tack every watch – every four hours – but the storm kept rising, and soon it blew a perfect hurricane. We had to take in more canvas, but we could not do much, for no sooner had we made one sail fast than another was blown out, thus we were working all the night and the next day without sleep. At last, the ship became unmanageable, all the canvas being blown away.

A big steamer hove into sight, and we hoisted signals of distress. It waited in the vicinity for hours, but did not come alongside, its captain evidently being afraid that our rigging might give way. With its departure our hopes sank, and we little expected that all of us would reach land again. We still had the foretopsail set, but that at length gave way, the chain breaking, and all went, the ship taking her own course. So we drifted before the gale and came here. We saw the Fleetwood lightship and a buoy, and then as we came nearer the shore we dropped anchor, but lost it. The port anchor was then let go.

It dragged, and so we came slowly ashore, otherwise the vessel might have gone to pieces before the lifeboat reached us. We showed a light, and the people on shore answered it. Then we knew that something would be done for us. We had put on our life belts, and if we had not thought that the lifeboat would come we intended to jump into the sea and try to swim ashore. It was suggested that our boat should be launched, but the captain was afraid to risk it, fearing it would not live in such a sea; besides, it would not have carried the whole crew.

The lifeboat reached us at nine o'clock, and when we landed we were very nicely treated. This is the second time I have been wrecked, but never before did I receive such hospitality as has been extended to us here. When was I wrecked before? Oh, in the Baltic, but the people did not treat us anything like this. Excuse me now – I must do some more packing up.'"

So the crew were well satisfied with their treatment thus far; but there was much more to come. Christmas was upon them, and of course the local populace could not let pass such an opportunity to demonstrate their hospitality to the bedraggled, but very likeable, seamen in their charge. Probably most of the crew had never had such a merry Christmas in their lives. Again, the reporter:

'The shipwrecked sailors will leave the Fylde with an exceedingly high opinion of Lancashire hospitality. Visitors to the neighbourhood generally call at the Red Lion where the men are still staying, and, of course, rarely depart without leaving them something of a "treat".

Mrs Hardman has shown herself particularly considerate in seeing to their comfort, and on Christmas Day she entertained them to a typical Christmas dinner of plum pudding, beef and turkey. The Vicar, Revd G. Leighton, kindly assisted the good lady by undertaking the duties of carver. The landlady, Mrs Castle, did herself credit by the way the dinner was served, and at the close Capt. Danielsen, on behalf of himself and his crew, thanked Mrs Hardman in simple and sincere language for her great kindness shown towards them by the people in the village. The crew had also accepted the Vicar's invitation to attend the Bispham church tea-party on Wednesday evening, where they were the objects of much attention, and where they appeared to enjoy themselves considerably. Most of the men are returning to Liverpool this weekend, with a view to obtaining employment upon other ships.'

The spiritual needs of the sailors were not overlooked, either. This article appeared under the heading 'Shipwrecked Mariners at Church'.

'An esteemed Bispham correspondent writes: "On Christmas Morning the usually quiet little church at Bispham presented a very interesting sight. Captain Danielsen, the mates, and several of the crew of the ill-fated barque attended Divine service, and their earnest and devout behaviour plainly demonstrated their gratitude for the merciful providence extended to them during the storm, in which so many others had found watery graves. As we have already announced, the captain and most of the crew were Norwegians, but several could read English, and the hymns seemed easy to them.

The people of Bispham will always cherish a kind regard for them on account of their exemplary conduct in civility and soberness. They have been most comfortably quartered at the Red Lion Hotel, under the care of Mr and Mrs Castle, and although visited and treated by so many sympathizing friends, not a single instance of excess or bad language has been witnessed. They are high in praise of the treatment extended to them on all sides. Some have been shipwrecked many times and in different countries, but they all agree that the kindness shown them here exceeds all."'

The ship's bell now rests in another church. Somewhere along the line Capt. Danielsen must have become friendly with the landlord of another hostelry, the Cleveleys Hotel. Mr Hindle was apparently the first locally to sense the impending disaster. The Cleveleys was much nearer the scene of the wreck than was the Red Lion; perhaps the captain had to stay around long after his crew departed, to complete the formalities with HM Receiver of Wrecks, and the Cleveleys proved to be a much handier place to work from.

Anyway, Danielsen ended up presenting the bell to Mr Hindle. There are reports that the captain had a dog, which he also gave to the landlord. Our worthy man-on-the-spot doesn't mention a dog, but then he couldn't be everywhere. Maybe it lay 'doggo' on the ship, miraculously surviving until the tide had gone out and then jumped ashore. A sea-dog is nobody's fool.

Mr Hindle was a founder member of the parish church of St Andrew, Cleveleys, so naturally the bell ended up there. There it still hangs, a little aloof, in the north-west porch. All told, everyone came out of the affair remarkably well.

The captain and the crew couldn't possibly have been blamed in the hurricane conditions; five ships were wrecked in Morecambe Bay alone on that particular night, one of them registered in the *Abana*'s home port of Farsund. She was another sailing ship called the *Valhalla*, and she was a total loss off Holyhead. So Captain Danielsen wouldn't have had very much explaining to do when he got home; in fact, he and his crew deserved all credit for beaching her so well. The lifeboat crew also got their deserved praise. They did a great deal of work during that storm, apart from the *Abana*.

The locals had a chance to show their unselfish hospitality, and were rewarded with a dog, a bell, and a tale to tell. The *Abana* was twenty years old when she struck that night. That is a respectable age for a ship, for working ships, like dogs, do not live as long as their masters. At that time, too, wood and sail were slowly and inevitably giving way to iron and steam. She would long since have been broken up in some anonymous yard, to be hacked to pieces and valued only for her timber by the foot.

I have been out to the wreck many times; it's only about 500 yards from the present day promenade. Only bare, truncated ribs are left, almost calcified by the tides which have washed over them in ninety years. Once I took a pocket knife and dug through the encrustations; the timber seems to be in excellent condition, considering the circumstances.

I have watched, too, the children around her. To some, it is a pirate ship and they dig in the sand for doubloons; to others it is a crashed space-ship in disguise. You see in their eyes each one making up his or her own story. I wonder how many boys have re-enacted the actions and commands of Capt. Danielsen, sailing with him before the howling hurricane, feeling the helpless ship quiver beneath their small feet, searching for the one order that will save the day. How many girls have been the imaginary captain's wife, clinging to him as he battles with the huge wheel and shouts incomprehensible orders into the driving spray? Here the *Abana* still sails, proud and tall, in the imagination of her children. Surely a happy resting place for any ship.

The writer is grateful for permission to use the sterling coverage of the incident by the *Fleetwood Chronicle, Fylde News and Advertiser* of 1894.

Ken Hardman, 1980s

This extract first appeared in a shipping magazine and is reproduced here with permission of Ken Hardman, who lives in Thornton.

Total Eclipse and Cockle Hall

A few weeks ago, accompanied by the fourteen-year-old son of a friend of mine and one of his friends, I walked from Stanah, Thornton, to Skippool and, when the route is walkable and not waterlogged, this is one of the finest local walks I know. We chatted about all kinds of things and the fourteen-year-old said that whereas he found it relatively easy to understand that light travelled at the speed of 186,000 miles a second, it was difficult for him to comprehend that heat travelled at the same speed. Oddly enough, when I was a boy I had the same difficulty until one day in 1927 when the issue became wonderfully clear to me.

On that day – I think it was in the early autumn but I can't be sure now – there was a total eclipse of the sun, something that had not been seen in Britain for over 200 years. I was then a schoolboy attending Baines Grammar School at Poulton-le-Fylde and arrangements had been made for us to walk from the school to the T-wood, which adjoins the railway lines, to watch the eclipse. Public transport started at an incredibly early hour that day and, as far as I remember, the eclipse, which lasted for several minutes, started at about 6 a.m.

Various national newspapers and magazines had presented free smoked glasses with which to watch the sun as it disappeared behind the moon and, equipped with my glasses and some bars of chocolate, I left home at an hour I hardly knew existed until then, caught a bus to Thornton station, then a train to Poulton and walked from Poulton station to Baines Grammar School, where I walked to the T-wood. It was, of course, a long walk, but this was in the days when people walked for pleasure. However mad it may seem to young people now walking was popular in those days.

We reached the T-wood – which is completely unchanged after all these years – and waited. Expectancy was in the air, and in the waiting moments as we peered through our smoked glasses we must have seemed like an assembly for some mountain-top ritual in pagan times.

A newspaper print of Cockle Hall. The hall was demolished just before the Second World War. This painting appeared in the *Gazette* in the 1950s.

As the sun disappeared it became intensely cold, proving that heat travelled at the same speed as light, and I remember the eeriness of the scene – the darkness, the cold and how the birds suddenly stopped singing.

After it was all over, we all seemed to be relieved – I certainly was because it seemed as if I had just emerged from an alien world – and we resumed chatting about the things that schoolboys of that era talked about: aeroplanes, cars, magazines, cigarette cards, fights, adventure and cowboy films. We were, as it were, back to earth again.

I explained all this to my two young companions and they seemed interested in my astronomy lesson. They afterwards asked me about the remains of the landing stage opposite Wardleys and I told them about the old ferry that used to cross the river there. I also told them about Cockle Hall which used to nestle behind the hawthorns at the bottom of the slope overlooking the ferry landing stage.

Alas, no carriage and pair ever swept up to the front door of Cockle Hall, no liveried retainer speeded the departing guests. Why it was ever called Cockle Hall I don't know, but it was like an old farmworker's cottage and it was bought by Thornton Cleveleys Council over thirty years ago and demolished.

The three of us inspected the site of Cockle Hall like Sherlock Holmes looking for clues in a murder hunt, and it is still possible to find the remains of a house. There are a few stone steps left and, among the brambles and weeds, can still be seen the legacy of what was once a garden.

Cockle Hall is a pleasant site in the summer, but it must be one of the loneliest parts of the Fylde in winter. I never remember it being occupied and in my young days there were stories about the place being haunted. It certainly looked more like a haunted house than anything else I have ever seen.

Why did Thornton Cleveleys Council buy it and then demolish it? There was no road there and there has been no development there since its demolition. The reason for its purchase and demolition brings us back to 1969. Cockle Hall was bought and demolished because the site lay in the path of the proposed new arterial road that some day, we were and still are assured, will cross the River Wyre at this point.

19 September 1969

Councillor J.H. Catterall presents National Fire Brigade first-aid certificates to members of Thornton Cleveleys fire brigade at the council offices.

Old Fire Brigade

The usual procedure now when anyone dials 999 and asks for the fire brigade in Thornton Cleveleys is for two brigades to attend, one from Fleetwood and the other from the Bispham fire station.

As one grows older, fires and fire engines seem to lose their excitement and with Thornton Cleveleys as it is now, most people don't know there has been a fire until they read about it in the local paper. In the old days when the siren sounded in the Council Offices yard at Thornton, one got the impression that the whole of Thornton Cleveleys had a personal interest in putting out the flames.

The first chapter in the history of organized fire-fighting in Thornton Cleveleys began with the formation of a brigade at the time when Thornton Cleveleys offices were at Rossendale Bungalow, now the Ashley Conservative Club. In those early days, most of the firemen were men from the United Alkali Company works at Burn Naze and when a fire occurred a bell tolled at the Council Offices and a telephone call was put through to the Burn Naze works.

Normally the local fire brigade dealt with haystack fires, but occasionally there was something more exciting. I remember, for instance, a fire at Gregson's Garage in Rossall Road which excited me so much that I was in danger of becoming a premature nervous wreck. Another fire I recall was at the Savoy Cinema, and I can remember the sky in the east aglow as if huge furnace doors had been opened when there was a fire at the United Alkali Works.

I can still, after all these years, recall the local firemen going into action. Out of Thornton Council yard would come a handcart, piled with hosepipes, and it would be manhandled to the scene of the blaze. Usually, Jack Rawcliffe had hold of the shafts, and Jack was a famous local character known to everyone. He normally drove the council's steamroller *Victoria* and, in his overalls and peaked cap, he was the envy of all small boys. As the council workmen made their way to the fire they would be joined by volunteers who seemed to enjoy the fire almost as much as we lads did.

At Cleveleys, adjacent to Beanland's Pavilion and now the site of the Home and Colonial shop, was a wooden hut containing all the Heath Robinson equipment then thought necessary for fighting fires. This, as far as I recall, stayed there until the mid-1930s.

With such a slap-dash approach to fire fighting in the old days, it wasn't usually long before some of the 'helpers' and spectators got a soaking. It was always great fun watching attempts to quell fires, especially farm fires, because when inexperienced handlers of hoses got to work there were fountains of water in all directions. Those, indeed were the days. When a bigger outbreak occurred the local firemen held the fort, as it were, until help arrived from outside the district.

On one occasion at a civic dinner at Fleetwood a councillor told an old joke which he jocularly attributed to Thornton Cleveleys Fire Brigade. He said that they had once turned out to a fire at Cleveleys and by mistake connected the hose to a gas main with the most remarkable results. This, of course, was a joke; it was told as a joke and intended to be received as a joke, but the story subsequently appeared in one of the national newspapers and, like Queen Victoria, our firemen were decidedly not amused.

The day when Thornton Cleveleys Council moved from a horse-drawn fire engine to a motorized one – a Model T Ford about which stories are legion – was a big step forward for the district. After that, even members of the council office staff would turn out for a ride on the fire engine when fires occurred during working hours.

As time went on, the brigade developed into a very smart organization and several times prizes were won in various inter-brigade tournaments and competitions.

Its peak period was in the last few years before the outbreak of war in 1939 and Thornton Cleveleys then had reason to be proud of its fire brigade. After the last war, small fire brigades with independent commands vanished because of re-organization and takeovers, and the fire service these days seems to be much more impersonal, however efficient it may be.

We knew all our firemen, mostly by their Christian names, in the old days, and there was no excuse for not knowing there was an outbreak of fire. The wail of the siren in the Council Offices yard ensured that everyone for miles around was well informed.

17 October 1969

The old fire station next to Beanlands Pavilion.

Terylene was Born in Thornton Cleveleys

As long as Thornton has been a name on the map – and it appears on all seventeenth-century maps – there have been farms there rich in local history. Some of these farms have dates carved on their walls or an odd crest or two and really old farms like Bourne Hall have local legends dating back to the days of the first Queen Elizabeth.

It is evident that at one time – up to the start of the nineteenth century – when folk here lived alongside the 670 acres of marsh and common land, that the bulk of the residents were squatters. These squatters were dependent on three large farms, Bourne Hall, Rossall Hall and Thornton Hall.

It was when the Lord of the Manor, then living at Rossall Hall, began to realize that if Thornton marshland was drained and tended it could be a much more profitable part of his estate, that things began to happen. The sequel was the Marsh Act of 1799. From that period

An aerial view of Hillhouse Works from a booklet promoting the factory.

Alkali Works, Thorton.

the district's fields and hedgerows, lanes, dykes and sea defences began to take shape. Soon afterwards, with a railway being laid and the town of Fleetwood springing up at the mouth of the River Wyre, Thornton found itself no longer a remote Fylde outpost.

Bourne Hall Farm's days of splendid isolation were numbered and now one can pass it and hardly notice it is there because, during the last ten years or so, it has been almost surrounded by the vast ICI Dyestuffs Division plant where work continues throughout the day and night.

Until about 1926 – that was the year when Thornton railway station moved from the south to the north of the level crossing – Bourne Hall was always referred to as Burn Hall and the ICI's Dyestuffs Division works was always referred to, and often still is, as the 'Burn Hall' works.

Thornton Cleveleys Council, for some reason I have never understood, decided that 'Burn Hall' should become 'Bourne Hall'. Nobody has ever been able to explain to me why the change was made, but the late Mr Bill Wright, Deputy Clerk to the Council, once told me that it stemmed from a road being renamed.

A short stretch of road by the farm used to be called Burn Road – it is now, of course, part of Fleetwood Road – and the council decided to change this name to Bourne Road. Bill Wright thought there might have been some confusion between Burn Road and Burn Naze or that councillors thought possibly that one Burn – Burn Naze – was enough. Not only was the name of the road changed, but the name of the farm also. I still don't know why a change was thought necessary in the first place.

Burn Hall, sorry, Bourne Hall, was an oasis for Fylde Roman Catholics in the days when they were being persecuted. Cardinal Allen, born at Rossall and christened at Bispham, certainly visited Bourne Hall and so did Edmund Campion, a Jesuit martyr, a life of whom was written by the late Evelyn Waugh.

The reason why Roman Catholicism has always been strongly established in the Fylde is that, despite persecution, the local Catholics were difficult to hunt out because most of the Fylde, like Thornton, consisted of marshland and swamp.

The old salt works, Burn Naze.

Many Roman Catholics 'on the run' used to stay at places like Bourne Hall where Mass was secretly celebrated, and those days are vividly brought to life in Evelyn Waugh's biography of Edmund Campion.

Bourne Hall is now, as I say, surrounded by the mammoth Dyestuffs Division works and in the last few years ICI have had a Thornton Cleveleys telephone number. In advertisements and official handouts, the ICI works at Thornton used to be referred to as the 'Fleetwood' works and they had a Fleetwood telephone number. In fact, only a relatively small part of the Dyestuffs Division plant is in Fleetwood and the whole of Mond and Plastics Division Works are in Thornton Cleveleys.

It was at the Hillhouse works, Thornton, that ICI, soon after the last war, introduced a pilot plant for the manufacture of a famous synthetic fibre called Terylene and advertised it extensively in its early days. These advertisements always annoyed me, and they also annoyed plenty of Thornton Cleveleys councillors and council officials, because they stated that Terylene was first manufactured at a pilot plant at Fleetwood. It wasn't.

It may seem very parochial to get steamed up over local boundaries and a few hundred yards of land, but let's get our facts right. Terylene, a word which everyone knows today, was born in Thornton Cleveleys and nowhere else.

31 October 1969

Cycling to Collect the Rates

As far as I know there has only been one instance in Thornton Cleveleys of a young man entering the service of the council, rising to a chief official's post and then, instead of 'getting his feet up' when he retired, contesting a council seat, winning it and devoting a great deal of the remaining years of his life to council work. That, however, was true of Cllr Tom Eaton who eventually became Chairman of the council and who died about ten years ago.

It was Mr Tom Eaton, as he then was, who told me more years ago than I care to remember that the present Council Offices in Fleetwood Road, Thornton, were originally built at a cost of £797 in 1905. From 1900, the year Thornton Cleveleys became an Urban District Council, until 1905, the Council Offices were in a bungalow at Rossendale Avenue, Thornton, now the Ashley Conservative Club.

The £797 represented the cost of the 1905 Council Offices and these, of course, have been added to substantially over the years. The new Council Offices were opened in May 1905, and present at the first meeting in the new building were Councillors Jude Crabtree – Crabtree Road is named after him – J. Titherington, T. Waring, T. Dewhurst, J. Gleeson, R. Bradley, W. Betney, T. Armitstead, and John Hall (Clerk), Henry Fenton (Surveyor) and Dr F.S. Rhodes (Medical Officer of Health).

There is quite a mystery surrounding one of the names just listed: John Hall, the Clerk of the Council. He afterwards went to London on business and disappeared completely, creating a local sensation that lasted for several years. Nobody knows what happened to him.

Matters dealt with at the first council meeting to be held at the new headquarters included a letter from a farmer at Stanah asking why the footpath to Wardleys Ferry had been diverted. Mr Henry Fenton pointed out that it had only been moved from one side of the fence to another, but it was decided to explain this in detail to the farmer who had written the letter.

An offer from Mr J. Croft, of Cleveleys, of 10s to use his boat during the season at Cleveleys foreshore was accepted. (Mr Croft and a boatload of passengers were all drowned on 1 September 1914, when there was a calm sea and no wind – another local mystery.) Councillor W. Betney strongly urged that there should be a railway station at Burn Naze. He said that he had been urging this for the past eleven years. A letter was read from the Lancashire and Yorkshire Railway Company stating that in future Thornton railway station – then called Cleveleys – would be called Thornton for Cleveleys.

One councillor said at this meeting that it had been an oversight on the part of the council in power when the Tramroad Company obtained their Act not to have a clause for a line to come down to Thornton, but the best story of those days I have heard – and it was told me by the late Henry Fenton – concerned Cllr Bill Betney, who lost an election because he advocated gas lighting.

He urged that Thornton Cleveleys should have its own gas works, but ratepayers found out – or alleged – that the cost would mean an increase of 2s 6d or 3s on the rates and they turned down Bill Betney's plea. It was in 1906 – the year after the new Council Offices in Fleetwood Road were opened – that the Thornton Gas Act of 1906 authorized the building of a gas works. For the next two years, until the Thornton gas works was built, Thornton Cleveleys got its gas supplies from Poulton-le-Fylde.

One of the first patrons of the new gas works off Butts Road, Thornton, was the Vicar of Thornton, the Revd C. N. Sergeant, who was getting tired of the oil lamps in use at Thornton parish church.

These were the days when the Council Offices acquired a new member of staff, Mr Tom Eaton, who was officially Assistant Overseer and Rate Collector, but the system of collecting rates in those days was very different from what it is today. In those days the rates were personally collected and it was Mr Tom Eaton's job to collect them and the gas accounts. Mr Eaton needed transport for his job, of course, and his transport consisted of a bicycle. His black collecting bag slung over his shoulder, Mr Eaton was a very familiar figure in the Thornton

Occupation Road, now Hawthorn Road – a typical Thornton scene.

Cleveleys of the old days cycling around the cottages and farms collecting the rates.

Mr Eaton in later years was fond of recalling his days on the bicycle and everyone then knew him. It was normal for him to be offered at least a cup of tea and he was, of course, expected to have a chat. In those days, the far-off days before the First World War, the population of Thornton Cleveleys was scarcely 4,000, so Mr Eaton had a good chance of personally knowing nearly all the local ratepayers.

The chief official of the Council Offices now is the Clerk, but until the mid-1930s Thornton Cleveleys had only a part-time clerk and the two principal officials were undoubtedly Mr Henry Fenton, the Surveyor, and Mr Tom Eaton, the Treasurer. Everyone knew them and they knew everyone. Imagine an official from the council's Treasurer's department calling round at one's house now on his bicycle to collect the rates, and afterwards sitting down to have a leisurely chat!

As the man with the deep voice used to say on the cinema screen, 'time marches on'. It certainly does.

How ICI Social Club Started

It was in May 1928, that the ICI Club at Thornton started, nearly two years after the merger of British Dyestuffs Corporation, Brunner Mond, Nobel Industries and the United Alkali Company to form the mammoth ICI combine.

The United Alkali Company started their Thornton works in the 1890s and a report in the *Blackpool Gazette and Herald* in April 1928 stated that 'one of the firm's first acts in the interests of the men's social side, after taking over the United Alkali Works at Burn Naze, Thornton, was to provide a much-needed social club for their workers... For this purpose, they have converted a commodious residence in Fleetwood Road, known as the "Manager's House", into an excellent club.'

Some of the pioneers of the new social club, those who were in 'at the ground floor' as it were, were well-known local men, such as Major Brunner, Messrs W.J. Lutyens, A. Taylor, H. Isherwood, A.J. Shaw and T. Dyson. These men must have been staggered to learn that the new ICI Club had an initial membership of 986. This huge membership presented a formidable and apparently insuperable problem for the opening ceremony in May 1928 and it was only solved by diverting the vast crowd into two assemblies, one in the old cricket pavilion, and the other in the club itself.

A smoking concert was held in both the cricket pavilion and in the new club, and Major G.H. Brunner, the chief engineer, presided over the gathering at the pavilion, supported by Messrs W.F. Lutyens, the general manager, Mr R.R. Wright, the assistant engineer, Mr R. Garron, Mr H. Maidment, the process manager, Mr E. Hilditch, the office supply manager, Mr W.F. Golden, engineer, and Mr A. Gregory, secretary of the new club.

An early view of the Alkali Works at Burn Naze.

Mr E. Percival, who had served with the United Alkali Company at Thornton for twenty-seven years, asked Mr Lutyens, the general manager, to accept a key with which to open the new club.

Mr Lutyens, who was very popular, said that when he and some of his colleagues came to Thornton ten months previously they had at once noticed the lack of a social club. He and his colleagues had been sent by the new ICI firm to 'pull the works together'. Then Mr Lutyens shocked his audience. If they failed to pull the works together, he said, the plant would be closed down altogether. He did not think there was much likelihood of this, he went on, but a great deal depended on the men themselves. ICI needed their help and their goodwill and Mr Lutyens regarded his first duty as 'to get hold of the men'.

Various improvements had been put in hand and the new club was not going to be run by the management for the men. That wasn't the idea at all. It was purely a working men's club whose members would form their own committees. The management would have one or two representatives on the committee with a watching brief, but that was all. It was a club for the men and it would be run by the men themselves, said Mr Lutyens.

Members present decided to send telegrams to Mr Henry Mond and Mr Watts, conveying best wishes and thanks for their efforts in getting a social club and, after the official opening by Mr Lutyens, Mr Walter Wood, an employee, presented a silver ashtray to Major Brunner to commemorate the opening 'and as a slight recognition of the kind and valuable assistance he has given towards the inauguration'. The whole assembled company then applauded Major Brunner and sang 'For he's a jolly good fellow', followed by three cheers.

After the opening ceremony, cricket, bowls, billiards and football section reports were submitted by Messrs A.J. Shaw – has anyone in the Fylde had longer connections with amateur cricket than Alf Shaw? – D. Connolly, F. Burne and T. Dyson respectively. Awards for the season were presented by Mr Lutyens and a vote of thanks to him was proposed by Mr E. Roach.

After the official business was all over there was a musical programme in the new club and songs were given by Messrs F. Wilde, G. Barker, A.J. Shaw, R. Fell, S. Cookson, G. Hylton and R. Wright.

In those far-off days of 1928, the then new ICI combine had only one works at Thornton, what was called the Alkali Works, belonging to ICI's Alkali Division. The old salt works was then being demolished and there is today nothing left of the old Alkali Works which was demolished four or five years ago. People now, naturally enough, associate the local ICI with the Hillhouse and Burn Hall Works, all of which originated on a very much smaller scale as Ministry of Supply factories during the last war.

The Burn Hall site in 1928 was a barren stretch of land occasionally used for grazing, and the site of what is now the Plastic and Mond divisions plants at Hillhouse was then farmland. What now houses huge retorts, main roads and various chemical works, in 1928 was the site of Starling and Hillhouse farms, two isolated farms apparently miles from anywhere. Even as late as 1928 it wasn't unusual to see an odd pheasant in that locality.

No pheasants are to be found there now.

9 January 1970

Damage caused by the 1927 flood on Cleveleys Promenade.

Memories of the Great Gales

I have an idea, though I may be talking through my hat, that gales used to be on a far more formidable scale than they are today. Reading old records tends to suggest that this is so, and most people over the age of about fifty probably believe as I do, that in the old days summers were hotter and the winters colder than they are today.

It was sometime in the late 1880s that a ship named *Janet Wignall* foundered near Dumfries and all hands were lost. The ship went down off Borness Shore and the tragedy was not made known until farm workers, passing along the beaches, saw pieces of timber from the wreck.

A local link with that sea tragedy of long ago was that the vessel's owner was named John Wignall, to whom the Methodist church in Victoria Road East, Thornton, is a memorial. It was given by his wife, Mrs Janet Wignall, after whom the ill-fated ship that sank while on a passage from Liverpool to Creetown, Kirkcudbrightshire, was named.

Mr Wignall was a leading figure in the shipping industry at Fleetwood for many years in the days when Fleetwood dealt chiefly with timber and grain cargoes, and he lived in Thornton or, rather, he lived during the summers in Thornton. His house was The Lawsons in Lawsons Road, Thornton, which was demolished to make way for new flats and garages. The Lawsons was believed to be around 300 years old and Lawsons Road was named after the house. Both Mr and Mrs Wignall were Methodists and, while living at The Lawsons, Mrs Wignall regularly attended the whitewashed Methodist church, long demolished, in Victoria Road.

This church was built in 1812 and it was the first Methodist church in the Fylde. It was through getting to know the Methodists there and realizing that this whitewashed cottage was too small and too unsuitable that Mrs Janet Wignall decided, years after her husband's death, to build a church at Thornton in his memory. The church that was built is, to give it its full name, the Wignall Memorial Methodist church.

I came across a photograph taken by my grandfather in 1929 of the *Commandant Bultinck*, an Ostend trawler which was wrecked off Rossall during a gale. In blinding rain, hail and thunder the trawler was returning to Fleetwood from a fishing trip after ten days at sea when she lost course, and despite the fact that her engines were going at full speed, the gale drove her towards the shore.

The trawler came ashore just north of Thornton Cleveleys boundary opposite what is now Westbourne Road or Shaftesbury Avenue with sirens wailing, and some of the crew could be seen clinging to the masts and others were huddled in the wheelhouse. It was night, the ship's lights were on and seen against a background of lightning the doomed vessel presented an eerie and frightening spectacle. Three members of the crew were drowned, overwhelmed by waves as they tried to get ashore. When the tide receded – this was around midnight – survivors lowered themselves by ropes over the side of the stricken vessel.

Masters and boys from nearby Rossall School played a big part in helping the survivors, especially those masters who spoke French. None of the crew could speak more than a few words of English and after spending the night at Rossall School they were taken to the Royal National Mission to Deep Sea Fishermen, in Dock Street, Fleetwood.

For weeks afterwards the wrecked trawler – a total loss, stranded high on the beach – attracted thousands of spectators, of whom I was one of the 'regulars'. However, it soon became difficult to approach the trawler, lying on its side, because of the overpowering stench of rotting fish.

Parts of the *Commandant Bultinck* were disposed of by its Belgian owners and after a month or two only a few spars remained as a souvenir of a night of terror and death. Eventually every bit of the trawler disappeared and long, long before the promenade was extended along that stretch of the coast, nothing remained to show that a trawler had foundered there.

The wrecked trawler fascinated me and I spent hours there, prying and peering until the stench drove me away.

The superintendent of the Cleveleys St John Ambulance Brigade for many years was the late Alf Parkinson, who had a herbalist's shop in Beach Road, Cleveleys. He had a large photograph in his shop of the wrecked *Commandant Bultinck* taken, I think, by himself.

By modern trawler standards, the *Commandant Bultinck* would be judged puny but, lying on her side, stricken and doomed, she looked like a great dinosaur in its death agony.

6 March 1970

34

The Great Fylde Flood

A few weeks ago I came across a photograph taken among the sand dunes that once extended in an almost unbroken line from Little Bispham to well north of the pumping station at Fleetwood. These sandhills were interrupted by Cleveleys Promenade, a primitive affair that, despite its shortcomings, served this district well until one fateful night in 1927. Cleveleys promenade was then battered out of all recognition and afterwards it was completely rebuilt in a totally different form.

What indescribably exciting places the dunes were for playing cowboys and Indians and all the rest of the games we played that seem to be unknown to the boys today! I remember the thrill of finding a dug-out in the dunes, not very far north of Beach Road. This, I subsequently discovered, had been built during the First World War and was occupied by somebody keeping a watch out to sea every night. It made a wonderful 'den' for years after it was officially abandoned.

In those days too, there was a large wooden building not far behind the sandhills and not far from the Beach Road Council School, as it used to be called. This was 'Beach Camp', which was inscribed in huge white letters that almost covered the entire roof, and it was fringed in summer by a score or more of bell tents. I think the camp was closed during the winter, but it was very popular during the summer months – a kind of motel, long, long before anyone had

Flood damage at Victoria Square, 1927.

Inspecting the damage caused by the flood of 1927.

heard that word. Soldiers often camped there during the summer.

Nearby was a big house, demolished before the last war, and this was Rossall Preparatory School, now the site of Jubilee Gardens. This building seemed curiously isolated then, especially during school holidays when it was – or seemed to be – totally deserted.

The entire Cleveleys Promenade was scarcely a quarter of a mile long and it finished abruptly opposite what is now the south entrance of Jubilee Gardens. It had old-fashioned, very Victorian-looking shelters. One was opposite Rough Lea Road, another at the top of Victoria Road and a third opposite Beach Road.

The tidal wave or waves that caused the 1927 flood smashed the old Cleveleys promenade to smithereens. Anyone who wants to see for themselves the extent of the flooding should look at the front entrance of the Strawberry Gardens Hotel, in Poulton-road, Fleetwood, where the depth of the flood waters is marked on a stone. This northern part of Fleetwood was affected worse than anywhere else and trams were unable to get through the flood waters although, oddly, the train service to and from Fleetwood continued, even though trains had to plough through flood waters near Wyre Dock.

An odd thing about the 1927 flood was that though huge areas of Fleetwood were inundated, parts of the town were completely unaffected. Areas around Bold Street and North Albert Street remained high and dry.

At Cleveleys, the flood waters came as far east as North Drive and the water was ankle deep at the old tram station which was in what is now Victoria Square. The flood waters stayed for weeks before they gradually subsided, leaving in their wake a mass of flotsam and rubbish.

At that time I was attending Baines' Grammar School at Poulton-le-Fylde and I travelled on the bus from Cleveleys to Thornton, on the train from Thornton to Poulton-le-Fylde and on my two legs from Poulton-le-Fylde to Hardhorn where Baines' School was and some of it still is. I travelled on the train with many Fleetwood boys and I well remember their graphic tales of the flood at Fleetwood.

To one of those Fleetwood boys, whose name was McCaffrey, I shall be eternally grateful because he once introduced me during a train journey to Greyfriars, the magically enchanting and never-to-be-forgotten world described weekly by the late Frank Richards in the pages of the *Magnet*, price twopence. He was one of those boys, a lad named Marsden was another, who told me of the Fleetwood disaster at first hand and of what could be seen from the train as it approached Wyre Dock station. Thousands of logs from the nearby sawmills were afloat, I was told, dead dogs were to be seen floating, people were marooned in their homes and so on. I thought those Fleetwood boys were exaggerating or having me on. It was only afterwards that I found out they were basically speaking the truth.

My father took a newspaper named *The Morning Post* then – who remembers that? – and the flood disaster at Fleetwood was extensively written about and there were photographs taken, I think, from boats. I suppose the flood featured prominently on the old 'steam' radio news, but I don't remember that.

I do remember the national appeal for victims of the flood at Fleetwood and I remember a wonderful old man telling me it all proved that other people were worse off than we were. That man was my maternal grandfather who was born in 1845, received a private education at twopence or threepence a week from an old soldier who had served with the Duke of Wellington during the Peninsular Campaign, and who had died, aged ninety, in 1935 as a result of falling off the roof of his house when he was repairing it.

13 March 1970

Mr Wilfred Ashley, MP for Blackpool.

A Famous MP Comes to Town

A few weeks ago I called to see the new extension and modernization schemes at the Ashley Conservative Club, Thornton, and I was suitably impressed though I, like many other people, regret the demise a few years ago of the delightful bowling green at the rear of the club. The Burn Naze Hotel and Cleveleys Hotel both had their own bowling greens and there was another delightful green at Enderley Gardens, Thornton, near the railway lines. All have disappeared and there are very few privately owned bowling greens here now.

It was in the spring of 1906 that Thornton folk heard martial music from the Poulton Brass Band as they marched along Victoria Road in front of an open carriage. In the carriage was Mr Wilfred Ashley MP, later Baron Mount Temple and father-in-law of Lord Louis Mountbatten, who came to Thornton to open a new Conservative Club named after him. Mr Ashley was MP for Blackpool – they had only one MP in those days – and he left the train at Poulton to ride to Thornton in an open carriage.

This proved to be a big day for Thornton because important people rarely visited the village, and when Mr Ashley arrived at the new club – at the junction of Alexandra Road and Victoria Road and now the site of a butcher's shop – there were speeches, cheers and afterwards lunch at the Gardeners Arms Hotel.

At the opening ceremony Miss Olive Boyd handed a buttonhole to Mr Ashley, and a key was presented to him by Alderman Bolton, a new Thornton resident and formerly of Oldham. Ald Bolton paid tribute to Mr Ashley's work as a Member of Parliament, and whilst he was referring to Mr Ashley's parliamentary majority a woman in the crowd shouted, 'It would have been more if women could have voted.'

The vote of thanks to Mr Ashley was proposed by Mr William Hodgson of Poulton-le-Fylde, later Sir William Hodgson. Major Greenwood, president of the Thornton Conservative Association, was to have presided, but he was taken ill at the last minute and Mr James Moore, vice-chairman, presided in his place.

Among those present were Messrs R. Hindle, J. Grimshaw, W. Atherton, E. Schofield, J. Titherington, R. Davidson, C. Whittaker, H. Boyd, T. Waring, W. Bramwell, J. Hall, R. Hull, J. Jolly, T. Walsh, S. Rimmer, W.H. Fox, L. Cohen, and J.T. Fair.

The Ashley Conservative Club moved soon afterwards to its present site at the junction of Rossendale Avenue South and Victoria Road East; this bungalow, previously, had been the site of Thornton Council Offices. The Ashley Conservative Club grew and prospered, as it still does, and a few years after its change of venue to the former council offices, a new name began to appear on the list of principal officials. From 1910 onwards the named of Mr Ralph J. Davies-Colley appeared. He came to live in Thornton in 1910 and he died in 1950 at the age of seventy-seven.

Mr Davies-Colley came from the Manchester district. He lived during his forty years in Thornton at The Hermitage in Victoria Road East, and he was manager of the Fylde Ice and Cold Storage Company in Fleetwood. He was a prominent local Conservative and a pioneer in the development of cold storage for the fishing industry. For some years he was a Thornton councillor.

What did Mr Davies-Colley have in common with a popular poet named Robert W. Service, born in Preston, and author of some famous 'pub' ballads, of which the best known is probably 'The Trail of Ninety-eight'? Robert Service, of course, had taken part in the famous Klondyke gold rush of 1898, but so, oddly enough, had Mr Davies-Colley, Thornton councillor, prominent local Conservative and a warden for many years at Thornton parish church. As a young man, Mr Davies-Colley had a real thirst for adventure, and on leaving Uppingham School his father gave him the choice of going to Cambridge or of taking a twelve-month trip around the world. Ralph Davies-Colley didn't hesitate; he chose to travel.

Later he was one of the first 500 prospectors in the Klondyke gold fields in Alaska. He endured appalling hardships and had some astonishing adventures there. On his return he was made a life member of the Royal Geographical Society.

Those who remember him will recall a smart, tall, debonair man with his back as straight as a plumb-line and a light, well-kept moustache. He was a businessman and he looked like a business man, but apart from those who knew him or who were aware of his background, nobody would have suspected for a moment that he had been a Klondyke prospector. He just didn't look the part, but that all goes to prove how deceptive appearances can be.

> Gold! We leapt from our benches. Gold! We sprang from our stools.
> Gold! We wheeled in the furrow, fired with the faith of fools.
> Fearless, unfound, unfitted, far from the night and the cold,
> Heard we the clarion summons, followed the masterlure – Gold!

That's a verse from Robert W. Service, whose poetry is still in print and apparently as popular as ever. Robert Service knew what he was writing about. He had endured the freezing cold of Klondyke, but so had Mr Ralph Davies-Colley, though nobody would have thought so when they saw him.

28 March 1970

A procession at Blackpool, including the Princess Louise, the Duke of Argyll and W.W. Ashley MP.

The Many Love Affairs of Vast Victoria

Thornton Cleveleys Parks Department deserve congratulations, all will agree, on the work they do at various local civic sites.

I attended the election count at Thornton Lecture Hall last week and I thought, as I entered the hall, that it won't be long before the gardens outside the Lecture Hall and library are ablaze with multi-coloured flowers, chiefly roses, and on the opposite side of the road are the war memorial grounds which are immaculately kept. I have heard hundreds, probably thousands of people praise the setting and layout of the war memorial grounds.

Four Lane Ends wasn't always like it is now, and it used to be a very quiet country crossroads. Old Thornton residents have told me of the excellent blackberries one could pick in the field – then called Strickland's field – where now stand the Lecture Hall and library. This, of course, was in the days before the bungalows, Villamar, The Hermitage and Ashdell, were built and the field belonged then to Rowlands Farm where Mr T.R. Strickland, Chairman of Thornton Cleveleys Council in 1904, farmed. Strickland's field is obviously named after Mr Strickland.

An old Thornton farmer, Mr John Walsh, who was born in Thornton in, I think, the 1840s, recalled the days when the pond in the ground of Villamar – still to be seen though very different from what it used to be – provided the Walsh family with their water supply when the cottage rain tub dried up. The Walsh family then lived in a cottage within a stone's throw of Four Lane Ends and their cottage finished its days as an outhouse in the garden of Marsh Heys – for long the home of Mr Hugh Butcher – and this was demolished in the 1920s to make way for vast new housing developments at Thornton in and around what is now Ullswater Avenue.

Before the war memorial grounds at Four Lane Ends were laid out in 1923, the crossing was dominated by Pointer House and on the opposite corner where Fourlands was built by Dr F.S.

The steamroller *Victoria* at work with some council employees.

Rhodes, Thornton Cleveleys' first Medical Officer of Health, there was poultry kept in an orchard by Jack Rawcliffe, a very famous local character.

Jack was in charge of the council's steam roller *Victoria* which, with steam hissing from its boiler, its mingled smell of coal and oil and its huge revolving fly-wheel, was one of the delights if my boyhood years.

It seemed vast and by modern standards I think it would still be regarded as vast. Its top speed, I suspect, was considerably less than walking speed and it had a tall chimney and a canopy which sheltered Jack from the rain.

Victoria was to be found almost anywhere in Thornton Cleveleys but wherever it was there were certain to be children around it, staring, touching and shouting to Jack Rawcliffe, but they were wasting their time. One might as well have tried to conduct a conversation near the Concorde when its jets are warming up.

I wonder, quite seriously, whether anyone who has ever lived in Thornton Cleveleys was better known than Jack Rawcliffe? I doubt it, but opposite Jack's orchard at Four Lane Ends lived another extremely well-known local character, Robert Swarbrick, the carter. His home was at Pointer House, now the site of the District Bank, and Pointer House was demolished about 1930 or soon afterwards when the appearance of Four Lane Ends was transformed. Pointer House, a white-washed building, was a farmhouse and Robert Swarbrick, known as 'Old Bob', was the chief local carter and contractor. 'Old Bob' or, to be more correct, 'Owd Bob', carted a great deal of material for the council long, long before there was a railway goods yard off Lawsons Road.

He carried bricks for the first house built in 1906 for the Cleveleys Cottage Exhibition, brought from St Annes the first oil lamps for Thornton roads and from Poulton and Fleetwood he carted material for the building of the Wignall Methodist church at Thornton.

'Owd Bob' came to Thornton from the Over Wyre district and he had worked at Hambleton for many years. Before living at Pointer House he worked for some time at Thornton Hall Farm. Bob Swarbrick liked to recall the days when his wages were 18s a week plus meals, and he paid 1s 6d weekly – yes, 1s 6d – rent for a house.

His parents farmed somewhere in the Over Wyre district – Hambleton I think it was – and as a youth he regularly got up at three o'clock in the morning to walk 12 miles to work. When he had finished work, he walked 12 miles back home. He died in the late 1920s or very early 1930s and in the old days he never, as far as I know or have heard, missed having a 'turn out' in the annual gala procession. Bob Swarbrick was a grand old character and despite his long working hours he looked as fit as a proverbial fiddle.

Yes, there was Bob Swarbrick at one side of Four Lane Ends and Jack Rawcliffe with his hens but minus his steamroller *Victoria* on the other side, opposite Bob Swarbrick's Pointer House. They were a couple of real characters and when I was a youngster I thought Jack Rawcliffe had the most wonderful job in the world. He was in charge of *Victoria*, he stoked the boilers, watched the pressures, oiled the machinery from a weird looking oil-can with a huge spout, and he was paid for all this.

I have no wish now to drive a steam-roller, but I wonder how many middle-aged men there are these days who are as content, as happy if you like, as Jack Rawcliffe or 'Owd Bob' Swarbrick? They worked hard for very little money and they brought up families from their meagre wages. Statistically they were underprivileged all right, but one would have to travel a long way to find a couple of men who were happier than these two.

15 May 1970

Anchorsholme Hall.

Anchorsholme Hall

A few years ago there died in Melbourne, Australia, a Mr A.A. Brunton who was born at Rossall in the 1880s and who emigrated to Australia before the First World War. He served with the Australian Army during the First World War and soon after the end of the last war he occasionally wrote fascinating letters to the *Thornton Cleveleys Times* about his boyhood days here. He was, I think, in his eighties then, but he had a remarkable memory and he wrote a script that would have shamed almost any teenager. His spelling and punctuation were impeccable and he recalled names and places with the greatest of ease. Mr Brunton used to recall the time in the 1890s when there were no buildings of any consequence between Rossall School and Anchorsholme Hall.

Everyone knows Rossall School, but Anchorsholme Hall was demolished about ten years ago. It overlooked the southern section of Cleveleys Hydro golf course, that part to the south of Anchorsholme Lane West, and when this part of the old golf course was turned into Anchorsholme Park, the last days of Anchorsholme Hall had begun.

It used to be a famous local landmark but in the 1920s and 1930s it became surrounded by houses and bungalows and it was then impossible to see it from the tram track at Anchorsholme crossing. Alas, this lovely old hall, 150 years old and rich in history, finished its days as flats before the demolition men moved in.

A reproduction of the first press mention of Cleveleys, 1783.

Anchorsholme Hall, near the bowling green, 1965.

DINING ROOM, CLEVELEYS COLLEGE

The dining room of Cleveleys College at Anchorsholme Hall.

Anchorsholme Hall was one of the oldest houses along this stretch of the coast and it was a school from 1926 until the last war, but its moment of great glory was when Princess Louise, fourth daughter of Queen Victoria, spent her honeymoon here.

The hall was built by Charles Inman, the founder of the Inman cotton line, based at Glasson Dock, at a time when Preston and neighbouring towns formed the hub of the cotton industry in Lancashire and sailing ships from the southern United States landed their cargoes of raw cotton at Glasson Dock. At Glasson Dock can still be seen the ruins of the first cotton mill in Lancashire. After the death of Charles Inman, Anchorsholme Hall became the home of Thomas Emmott, a famous cotton magnate, whose son Charles (later Lord Emmott, Deputy Speaker in the House of Commons) married Constance Harriett, daughter of the Duke of Argyll. John, the brother of Constance, married Princess Louise, and that is how Anchorsholme Hall became the scene of a Royal honeymoon.

This part of the Fylde was then picturesque in summer but indescribably lonely in the winter and the nearest big houses to Anchorsholme Hall were Norbreck Villa, now Norbreck Hydro, and Eringo Lodge, subsequently Cleveleys Hydro, which was demolished twelve years ago and which, in 1875, was the home of Alderman John Cocker, Blackpool's first mayor.

Not many years before Anchorsholme Hall was built, the following advertisement apppeared in a Manchester newspaper:

'Anthony Salthouse, at Cleaveles, two miles from Poulton and two miles from Blackpool, begs to inform his friends and the public in general that he has very good accommodation for company during the bathing season at the above place. Those ladies and gentlemen who please to favour him with their company may depend on every effort in his power to render the situation as agreeable as possible.'

In 1926, Anchorsholme Hall was bought by Cllr J.H. Smythe, who turned it into a private school. He had about 100 pupils, mostly boys, but at the beginning of the last war in 1939 the school was closed.

Anchorsholme Hall comprised altogether thirty-three rooms with the entrance hall fitted out as a replica of one of the Irish cotton ships of Charles Inman. Boat-shaped, this hall was huge by present-day standards, and it had side rooms and alcoves which, as intended, gave a strangely ship-like effect. The ceiling was of heavy oak beams and on the walls were heads of deer, stags and gazelles. There was a superb black oak sideboard, elaborately carved, and along the panelling over the long mirror was the date 1692. Most of the alcoves contained statues.

It must be about twenty-five years since I was last in Anchorsholme Hall but I remember its interior vividly, especially the marvellous carved sideboard, surely one of the oldest – and finest – pieces of furniture in this district. I remember Cllr Smythe once telling me that he had examined this sideboard carefully and, as far as he could see, not a single nail had been used in its construction.

From the outside, Anchorsholme Hall didn't look particularly impressive. It was big and that was about all. One had to go inside to realize what a wonderful old hall is was. I well remember the days when it stood like a sentinel at Anchorsholme with no other buildings around it. On the east, of course, it was surrounded with fields, and there were a few white-washed cottages on the west side of the tram track at what is now Anchorsholme Crossing tram stop.

Cleveleys Hydro and Anchorsholme Hall have both been demolished and not a stone exists to remind one now of their existence. Both of them enshrined an enormous amount of local history and I, for one, was genuinely sorry to see them disappear. Both of them had character and I believe that some buildings, like some people, have a character all of their own. An important chapter of local history closed when these two old halls were finally demolished.

24 July 1970

Plenty of Perks for the Stationmaster

In my young days the old station house adjoining Thornton railway station attracted little attention and for long it was the home of Mr John Singleton, one of the porters at Thornton Station. For many years the Bay Horse Hotel, Baines' Endowed School and the station house formed a triangle alongside the stream that used to be the boundary between Thornton and Little Thornton. I suppose these three buildings must have had quite an air of importance once upon a time when they were surrounded by fields and farms. For most of its life, the station house was the home of Thornton stationmasters though I certainly don't remember any of them living there; that happened well before my time.

Probably the most famous of all the Thornton stationmasters was Mr John Billington and he lived at the station house for about thirty years from 1870 until the turn of the century. When he came to Thornton from Kirkham in 1870, house, coal and light were free and he was paid 18s a week. There was as much land as he could cultivate for use as a garden and he soon discovered that local people were generous and they gave him poultry and game. There was, of course, plenty of time between trains to do his gardening and the stream was admirable for the ducks he bred.

In those days, Thornton had a reputation as a meeting place for Quakers and it was usual to see some of the Quakers around the district. One of them was an old Thornton farmer name John Walsh who lived at Marsh Farm and who was born in Thornton in the 1830s. He lived until the 1920s and though I never met him, an old friend of mine, the late Desmond Lewis of Thornton, knew him well and had spent hours chatting with him.

John wore the broad-rimmed Quakers' hat and he kitted milk to Liverpool. The first morning Mr Billington was on duty at Thornton, John said to him: 'Tha mun get two kits. If tha will laden ma milk cans int' trains I'll keep tha in milk.' John brought him a quart of milk every morning, leaving his big cans to be put on the train.

There were all sorts of gifts for the Thornton stationmaster in those days in return for the kindnesses he was able to do for the farmers. During the summer he received untold baskets of fruits. Sometimes, when they were en route to Fleetwood market, farmers would bring their baskets and sacks on Thursday nights and Mr Billington kept them at the station until the following morning for the womenfolk to take on the train to Fleetwood.

Thornton station – then on the south side of what is now the level crossing – had a platform only a foot high in Mr Billington's time and attached to the house was a booking office and a waiting room made of railway sleepers. Mr Billington's job was for seven days a week – after all he did receive 18s a week wages – although sometimes there were no more than three or four passengers a day. The money Mr Billington collected was banked at Fleetwood every morning and often there was no more than two or three shillings.

The big snag then was the level crossing, a crossing that has exasperated impatient motorists ever since. These gates had to be opened by hand and there were times when Mr Billington had to use his ingenuity to get enough sleep. After the late train had gone through to Manchester he would close the gates to traffic so that the engine returning from Manchester could get safely through. To make sure the engine had passed while he was asleep, he placed cinders on the metal and if he found them crushed he opened the gates to road traffic and slept until the first train in the morning from Fleetwood was due.

On one memorable occasion, bees entered the station house, John Billington's home, apparently through a ventilator, and carried on their business about the joists between a bedroom floor and the ceiling below.

This, I understand, went on for a couple of years or so and then – yes, it was bound to happen – the queen bee left the hive and the thousands of her subjects swarmed to the front of the railway station and gave intending railway passengers the fright of their lives. However, help was soon on its way. An engineer from Fleetwood railway sheds – demolished only a few years ago – who kept bees was sent for and he persuaded the bees to return to a hive. This wasn't the end of the story. One swarm had followed their queen and left John Billington's house, but swarms, I understand, are caused by

Old and new stations, 1926.

there being two or more queens. Some of the bees and their queen remained in Mr Billington's house. Part of a bedroom floor was cut away to find them and get the honey out. The part that had been cut out was then covered with glass so that the bees could be seen at work. The length of the honeycomb between the joists was supposed to be 6ft. Old John Walsh saw it and that's what he said. The last bees – those that had stayed in John Billington's house – stayed there for another year or so and then, unaccountably, they seem to die off. Anyway, they didn't swarm outside.

In those far-off days there was no railway station at Burn Naze – that was built in the early years of the twentieth century – and the railway station was nothing like the station that is to be seen now and that was built in 1925. Alas, now we haven't a railway service at all or, rather, we don't have a passenger railway service.

It's enough to make old John Billington turn in his grave.

31 July 1970

REARED AT CLEVELEYS.

The Famous

" CHAMPION CONN," of Cleveleys,

Who holds an international reputation. Winner of 25 Championships.
This record has never been equalled by any Dane in any part of
the world. ∴ ∴ ∴ ∴ Young Stock always for Sale.

STUD FEE, £4 4s.

· Apply: Kennel Man, The Towers, Thornton-le-Fylde.
Telephone 22, Cleveleys.

An advertisement for a 'stud' at Mr Kirwan's 'Old Firm', 1913.

Mr Kirwan's Great Dane

In April 1783, six years before the start of the French Revolution, a couple of years before Ralph Slater built Marsh Mill at Thornton – and a similar mill at Pilling – and a year or two before Cartwright invented a revolutionary power loom for spinning, a Mr Anthony Salthouse, of Manchester, wrote a letter to a Manchester newspaper. He 'begged leave to inform his friends and the public in general' that he had very good accommodation for company during the bathing season at a place called 'Cleaveles.' Though Thornton was first mentioned in the *Domesday Book* as Torentum, this is almost certainly the first mention of Cleveleys as distinct from Thornton.

This was recounted in a booklet which was issued in 1952 by Thornton Cleveleys Council. It was entitled *Walks and Tours In and Around Thornton Cleveleys*, and though it is now well and truly out of date, it was in its time a very valuable reminder that Thornton Cleveleys consisted of more than a promenade and a shopping centre. Most of the walks described were over fields that long ago disappeared to give way to housing development.

The booklet contained all kinds of out-of-the-way information about this district. How many people, for instance, know that the first cargo of cotton for Lancashire spinning mills from the Southern States of American arrived at Wardleys, directly opposite Stanah, or that, little more than a century ago, over 400 Roman coins were discovered near Rossall School, the site of which was, in the early sixteenth century, the birthplace of Cardinal Allen?

The booklet contained an interesting theory that the seaboard strip of Thornton became known as Cleveleys because a man of that name kept the old Cleveleys Inn. Whether that theory is true or not I don't know and nobody else knows. What cannot be disputed, however, is that there used to be an inn on the corner of what is now Rough Lea Road and North Promenade. This was the main coastal road to Fleetwood more that 100 years ago. As there were then no full-scale sea defence works, only an improvised cobblestone slope, the sea washed over so often that this coastal road had to be abandoned in favour of what is now Rossall Road.

The late Mr Fred Goddard of Henley Avenue, Cleveleys, a man with a remarkable knowledge of old Thornton Cleveleys, once told me that when the road originally called Garfield Road and afterwards North Promenade was being built, workmen excavated part of the old cobbled coastal road.

After Rossall Road had replaced this old coastal road, Cleveleys Inn became a house, and Mr M.B. Kirwan, then recently returned from Australia, bought it as his home. He bred huge Great Dane dogs in kennels adjoining the inn, and Mr Goddard, who knew him well, told me of his skill with a long stock whip. He exercised his dogs daily and nearly a couple of dozen of them would walk ahead of him, none of them on leashes. If any of them became quarrelsome or frisky, Mr Kirwan would produce his stock whip, which had a very short handle and about 20ft of leather, whirl it through the air in the best John Wayne, wild-west cowboy manner, and crack it a few inches from the misbehaving dog.

Mr Goddard, who used to work at the Surveyor's Department at Thornton Cleveleys Council Offices, once told me about visiting Mr Kirwan at the inn. He walked in and was asked to wait for a minute. Suddenly he felt something cold and snake-like caressing his neck. It was the end of the stock whip and Mr Kirwan was giving a practical demonstration of his skill with it. He pointed out to Fred Goddard what he could have done with his stock whip if he had been an unwelcome intruder, instead of a friend.

If a thief were stupid enough to break into the inn, Mr Kirwan, unaided by his Great Danes, was sufficiently skilled with his stock whip to ensure that the intruder would have left, as it were, with 'his head tucked underneath his arm'.

Soon after the turn of the century, Mr Kirwan left Cleveleys Inn for The Towers, off Holmefield Avenue, afterwards Highfield College and, in the last few years, acquired by the council. I remember once going with my father to The Towers, where there used to be a large fig tree growing outside the main door, and being suddenly confronted by half a dozen baying Great Danes. A million assurances wouldn't have convinced me that these huge animals were docile and harmless. They looked like a nightmare come to life and they terrified me. I don't think I could have been more frozen with fear if I had suddenly encountered a hissing, 15ft king cobra with its hood extended.

After Mr Kirwan left Cleveleys Inn it was unoccupied for some years and then it became a photographic studio, the Ruskin Studio. More than forty years ago it was demolished and the site was occupied by Mr Albert Mason's amusement arcade. Where once coaching parties stopped and the scene, one likes to think, was like a Christmas-card view, there are now slot machines and bingo.

The present building is called Olympia and has children riding on mechanical donkeys, scores of slot machines – what happens to them when decimal coinage is introduced next February? – ice-cream, lollipops and bingo callers shouting 'Downing Street', 'Key to the Door', and so on. How odd it is to realize that this was the site of an eighteenth-century coaching inn.

Whether or not a 'Mr Cleaveles' was ever 'mine host' at the inn I don't know. I remember the building in its last, sad days as a ramshackle, dilapidated old place with the name 'Ruskin Studio' barely decipherable on a rotting nameplate. It didn't look much like an inn then, but it looks even less like an inn now.

I'll bet it was an eerie and spooky place in winter when gale-force winds lashed the sea to fury and the waves crashed over the cobble-stoned sea defence and pounded the old inn. Anyone inside the inn would, naturally, have been scared but I doubt they were as scared as a schoolboy in short trousers long, long ago, when he stood at the main entrance to The Towers without a care in the world one minute and seconds later, half a dozen Great Danes pounded out, seemingly intent on terminating a life that had scarcely begun.

30 October 1970

The Steel Monster

As long as I live I suppose I will continue to regret the closure of Thornton railway station because, in one way or another it played quite a part in my life.

Before 1926, when the station was south of the level crossing, I remember welcoming and saying goodbye to various aunts and uncles; in 1926 I had a contract between Thornton and Poulton-le-Fylde when I started attending Baines' Grammar School, and in March 1940, at the end of the severest winter I remember – the sea froze over and the tram service had to be suspended – I left Thornton station to join a famous infantry regiment.

For more than two years I soldiered in this country and Northern Ireland and I can recall leaves from Lisburn and Omagh in Ulster, from Brecon, Cottenham, near Cambridge, Guildford, Esher and Woking which had one thing in common: I either arrived home via Thornton station or left from there.

Most people in Thornton Cleveleys seemed genuinely sorry to see the end of Thornton railway station and an impressive number of local organizations fought hard to prevent its closure. To me, for obvious reasons, Thornton wasn't merely a railway station; a great deal of my life was, in one was or another, connected with that station.

How many people, I wonder, know that the Preston to Fleetwood railway was one of the oldest in Britain and that it was opened in 1840, only five years after the Stockton and Darlington railway line – the first passenger railway in Britain?

The loop line from Preston to Lytham and Blackpool was not opened until 1846, and until then holidaymakers for Lytham St Annes and Blackpool had to leave the train at either

Outside the new railway station, which was also the bus terminus, in 1926.

Kirkham or Poulton-le-Fylde and then make their way by coach. The Preston-Fleetwood line was opened on 25 July 1840, partly because of the urgent need of Fylde farmers to get their produce to Preston market, and also because of the rapid growth of a new town at the mouth of the River Wyre. Though the first house had been built at that new town only in 1836, the place was developing rapidly, chiefly as a fishing port.

Until 1836 it had no name except The Warren, presumably because of the large number of rabbits there, and it was decided to call the new town after the name of the local Lord of the Manor, Sir Peter Hesketh Fleetwood, Member of Parliament for Preston. Sir Peter lived at Rossall Hall, afterwards the site of the Northern Church of England School, which changed its name to Rossall School over a century ago. Sir Peter's estate, by the way, included most of what is now Cleveleys and Anchorsholme and he built the first sea defences at Cleveleys. He liked to tour around his huge estate in what I think was called a 'gig' – or was it a 'fly'? – drawn by an immaculately groomed pony.

During the week ending 14 December 1842, 911 passengers travelled on the Preston-Fleetwood line, and by 1846 the weekly figure had increased to 2,820. In those days there wasn't a stop at Thornton or Burn Naze – the only stops were Preston, Kirkham, Poulton and Fleetwood. The Thornton stop was introduced in the 1870s and the Burn Naze stop – the United Alkali Works arrived here in 1893 – wasn't built until 1903. The fare from Preston to Fleetwood was 4s 6d first class, 3s second class and 2s third class. There were three trains a day from Fleetwood to Preston and back and one on Sundays.

Until 1840 – three years after a young girl named Victoria came to the throne – there were three ways of travelling: on foot, on horseback or by coach. The *Rocket* type of locomotive must have flabbergasted farmers in the fields as it thundered by at, I suppose, around 40 miles an hour. One local man of letters, Mr Henry Anderton, was so moved by the sight of the steel monster that he burst into verse for the occasion. After an initial tribute to Sawney McAdam, the famous road engineer, from whom we get the word 'macadam', comes the peroration:

The present has taken great strides from the past
For carriages run without horse at last!
And what is more strange – yet it's truth I avow,
Hack-horses themselves have turned passengers now!
These coaches alive go in sixes and twelves,
And once set in motion they travel themselves!
They'll run thirty miles while I'm cracking this joke,
And need no provisions but pump-milk and coke!
And with their long chimneys they skim o'er the rails,
With two thousand hundredweight tied to their tails
While Jarvey in stupid astonishment stands,
Upturning both eyes and uplifting of hands,
'My nags,' he exclaims betwixt laughter and crying,
'Are good 'uns to go, but yon devils are flying.'

That's what they thought of the new railway – flying devils, and it's a safe bet that plenty of people in those days argued that if the good Lord had intended people to travel by rail he'd have put tall chimneys on their heads.

In 1847, a disastrous year for this country as there was a severe potato famine and real starvation among the poor – these were the 'hungry forties' and the days of the Chartist movement – the young Queen Victoria, recently married to a German, Prince Albert, visited the new port of Fleetwood.

The royal couple arrived in the Royal Yacht *Britannia* after they had toured Scotland, and *Britannia* anchored for one night off Fleetwood. The visit is mentioned in Queen Victoria's famous diary, her 'best-seller' entitled *Leaves from our Highland Journal*, published in 1868.

New station, 1926.

Apparently it was a rough night and *Britannia* was heavily buffeted. The next morning the royal party came ashore at Fleetwood and boarded the royal train back to London.

There was, as I have mentioned, no station at Thornton in 1847 when the royal train passed through, but it's a safe bet that the locals knew what was afoot and I'm sure they gave a cheer as the train thundered at top speed through Thornton.

Is it any wonder that after all its long history, so many local people were saddened and grieved at the passing of Thornton railway station and the withdrawal of passenger services between Poulton-le-Fylde and Fleetwood? For the last few years before its closure, of course, local trains were diesel-powered, and I neither know nor care how much more efficient on a power-weight ratio they were or are than steam locomotives. If they were a million times more efficient I would still say that steam engines have, like some old towns and cities, souls of their own. Diesels haven't.

I can't understand any man or boy staring with love, reverence, awe and admiration at a soulless hunk of metal like a diesel locomotive, but I can easily understand how men will, whatever the inconvenience, make a pilgrimage to see steam locomotives brought out of retirement for inspection and trial runs. I have, like most people, seen plenty of banality, brutality, boring plays and unadulterated rubbish on television, but not all that long ago I saw on the 'telly' the genuine, the one and only *Flying Scotsman* brought out of retirement for a high-speed exhibition run. I decided there and then that what I had just seen was well worth a year's television licence fee.

27 November 1970

Victoria

When I was a small boy I envied people, men like Douglas Fairbanks Snr, Tom Mix, Milton Bills, Jack Dempsey and so on, but these were men in two dimensions. As far as real, three-dimensional men were concerned, I suppose I envied most of all Jack Rawcliffe who was in charge of *Victoria*, but *Victoria* was no lady.

In 1900 when Thornton Cleveleys became an urban district council and the council offices were what is now the Ashley Conservative Club at the corner of Victoria Road East and Rossendale Avenue South, one of the first loans they obtained was to buy a steam roller, and so began *Victoria*'s long and distinguished career here, for this 12-ton monster took the name of the reigning monarch and she carried an inscribed plate which made her royal name known to all who passed by. Plenty of Thornton Cleveleys boys looked with envious eyes on the steam roller's driver, Jack Rawcliffe, who drove *Victoria* from 1900 until his retirement in about 1932.

One of the remarkable things about *Victoria* was that after she had been helping, as tenors sing, to 'make the crooked straight and the rough places plain' for many, many years, it was suddenly discovered and by accident that a road licence had never been taken out on her. Motor cars and similar expensive novelties were so scarce when *Victoria* first came to Thornton that nobody thought about a road licence and so, year after year, she rumbled along her stately way until the omission was revealed. As the Lancashire County Council authorities saw the humour of the situation, all was well, and *Victoria* was able to go to her retirement without a blot on her escutcheon. Like some demobilized soldiers, she had 'exemplary' on her discharge certificate.

Victoria, naturally, was the pick of the municipal stables and no matter how great and glossy were the handsome horses that pulled the council carts around, none made such an impressive exit from the council yard as the royal lady *Victoria*, and many was the time when a man with a red flag walked in front of her to make sure that nobody got under her feet, so to speak.

The late Henry Fenton, surveyor to Thornton Cleveleys Council from 1900 until his retirement in 1940 – he was also, for most of that time, building inspector, chief of the fire brigade, gas manager and chief public health officer – told me that *Victoria* came from Norfolk in 1900. She was put in the charge of Jack Rawcliffe, a Marton man, who had driven a steam roller at Blackpool before he came to Thornton. Jack, as everyone called him, looked after *Victoria* with loving care, knowing just how to get the best out of her, even when she was temperamental. He was quite a friendly chap, his light blue smock and peaked cap giving him a sort of uniform without which a steam-roller driver would have seemed improperly dressed.

Victoria had a huge exposed flywheel which whirred round at what seemed a fantastic speed, and she smelt of a mixture of lubricating oil and steam – an irresistible combination for any boy – and I suppose that her top speed, when stoked up with good-quality coal, must have been at least four miles an hour.

Jack Rawcliffe was up at 5.30 every morning except Sunday to get the engine ready for turning out with the roadmen at seven o'clock. At one time the council had a stone breaker which was driven by *Victoria*, and Jack and his colleagues one day got through nearly 70 tons of stone – a feat which earned them a bonus and which, long afterwards, Mr Henry Fenton told me about. The stone breaker weighed over 10 tons, but *Victoria* could – and did sometimes – haul it through Kirkham and the roads there are far steeper than anything we have on the Fylde Coast.

Jack Rawcliffe lived at the house in Victoria Road next to the Westminster Bank, formerly the District Bank, at Four Lane Ends. His back door looked out on the shippons and stables behind whitewashed Pointer House where Mr Bob Swarbrick, the carrier, lived for many, many years. Pointer House was demolished about 1930. Jack Rawcliffe's farming activities were confined to keeping poultry, although his wife really looked after the hens, and their run – all hens were 'free range' then – was the orchard across the road which belonged to Dr F.S. Rhodes. Dr Rhodes, Thornton Cleveleys' Medical Officer of Health, lived for many years in Woodland

Victoria pulling up trees at Four Ends Lane in 1938, the year the Lecture Hall and Library opened.

Avenue, Thornton, and he built Fourlands at Four Lane Ends. The pear tree that dominated the orchard has long since been dwarfed by the development of Four Lane Ends.

Jack Rawcliffe and *Victoria* retired at about the same time and it was a partnership that will be affectionately remembered by everyone who remembers Thornton Cleveleys as it was in the old days. Jack went to live in High Furlong and the council wrote to him enclosing a resolution passed at a full council meeting stating that the twelve Thornton Cleveleys councillors tendered their best wishes for his good health and long life in retirement. They also placed on record their recognition of his exemplary service to the council for over thirty years as the driver of *Victoria*. The two of them were inseparable.

As a small boy I followed *Victoria* for miles and she must have covered countless times every yard of road in Thornton Cleveleys during her career, including all kinds of roads that were then, and are still, little known. *Victoria* would be lost in the Thornton Cleveleys of today, and so, alas, would her master Jack Rawcliffe, to whom I waved hundreds – or was it thousands – of times on days long ago.

18 December 1970

The Holiday Guide

Given a reasonable degree of co-operation, the final touches should be given soon to the 1971 guide for Thornton Cleveleys and copies of this will, as usual, go to individual enquirers, to firms, travel agencies and certainly to some very strange, far away places. I don't suppose that copies of our official guides have ever reached Greenland or Communist China, but they have been sent to just about every other country in the world.

The story of our holiday guides goes back to 1913 when the first guide was issued, published by Cleveleys Ratepayers' Association, price one penny. One of those primarily responsible for compiling it was the then new headmaster of the Beach Road Council School, Mr J.H. Catterall. The school was opened in 1906 by Mr William Hodgson, of Poulton-le-Fylde, afterwards Sir William Hodgson, chairman of Lancashire County Council, and Mr Catterall was its first headmaster and remained in the post until the late 1930s.

He became a councillor in the 1930s and was chairman of the council in 1938 and 1939. He lived in Cleveleys Avenue with his wife and his mother-in-law, who celebrated her 100th birthday during the last war. Mr Catterall was one of the founders of Thornton Cleveleys Old People's Welfare Association in 1946 and he died twenty years ago. After devoting most of his working life to the interests of boys and girls, he turned his energies for the last twenty years or so of his life to the problems of old people.

The Cleveleys that the first publicity guide of 1913 describes is unrecognizable today, and it is almost impossible when reading the 1913 booklet to realize that it is describing Cleveleys. Fields, dykes, farms, sandhills, hawthorn-hedged country lanes, a simple cobble-stoned sea defence and promenade plus a few houses: that was the kind of district the 1913 guide was determined to publicize and popularize.

This was Cleveleys where a motor car was a real novelty and local tranquillity and peace reflected the national sense of stability and prosperity that existed for most people in that now

Beach Road School, c. 1910.

Map of Thornton Cleveleys.

remote world of 1913.

The population of Thornton Cleveleys was then 5,000 and the compilers of the 1913 guide were at pains to stress the natural and unspoilt aspects of this district. A new promenade had been built that year 'but it is no disfigurement to the place – as unfortunately so many artificial promenades are – being just a strip 12ft wide of beautifully smooth walking. It is nearly a quarter of a mile long and ends just where the snuggy sand dunes begin.' That promenade lasted from 1913 until 1927 when it was smashed to smithereens by a great storm and Cleveleys and Anchorsholme were extensively flooded. The floodwaters extended as far inland as North Drive, but the worst affected areas were around Stanley Road and Ash Street at Fleetwood.

Twelve years before the first official guide of 1913 was issued there were no churches in Cleveleys, though Thornton had no fewer than four churches. In 1909 the Cleveleys Park Methodist church was built, St Andrew's parish church was built in 1910 and the original Congregational church was built in 1902.

One of the most fascinating aspects of the 1913 guide is, inevitably, the illustrations. There is a photograph of the then new promenade showing ladies in Edwardian-style boaters and sunshades watching Mr Stratton Wells and his company of pierrots on the foreshore. This, and many other photographs, were taken by Mr Richard Sykes. Mr Sykes was a well-known amateur photographer, had the first chemist's shop in Cleveleys, the site afterwards of Messrs Timothy Whites, and he was a prominent member of and worker for St Andrew's church. Another photograph shows one of the old 'toast-rack' type trams which have long since disappeared from service, and the advertisements offer today's reader a rich reward, especially those that quote prices.

Long before Butlin's, two local brothers, J. and R. Wilkinson, had a men's camp off Beach Road. This opened in 1910 and was advertised as 'the very best holiday for men'. It cost 21s a week for full board.

A day trip from Fleetwood to Douglas by RMS *Viking* cost 4s 6d steerage or 6s 6d saloon.

Mr W. Doody, who had a grocer's shop next to what is now Tesco supermarket, advertised his 'noted tea' at 1s 6d and 1s 8d a pound, and those who liked alcoholic drinks were well catered for.

Mr W. Mann, landlord of the Cleveleys Hotel, advertised Bass and Guinness at 2s per dozen bottles. Mild and pale ale were 2s 6d per dozen large bottles or 1s 6d per dozen for small bottles.

One of the best-known characters in those days was Will Beanland, well known in stage circles as a pantomime 'dame', and he was for many years the licensee of the Old Pavilion Theatre, afterwards a cinema, in Victoria Road, near Victoria Square. In addition to concert parties at the Pavilion during the season, he advertised a special novelty: cinema shows. At that time the Palace Theatre (afterwards the Savoy Cinema) was not built.

The 1913 official guide contained a two-page inset map of the district prepared by Mr Henry Fenton, the council's surveyor, who was also the building inspector, gas manager, chief public health inspector and superintendent of the fire brigade. This map graphically illustrates the vast changes that have transformed Thornton Cleveleys out of recognition.

In 1913 gas lighting was a novelty here and boarding-houses advertised that their rooms were lit by gas – there was no electricity supply in Thornton Cleveleys until 1926 – but despite this apparent backwardness there were many compensations, chief of which probably was a real community spirit. Everybody seemed to know everybody else. Going shopping or going for a walk was invariably one long succession of 'good mornings' and 'good afternoons' to people one knew.

Though we lacked many amenities, and boasting of a gas supply makes us smile today, we must have had something to recommend us as a holiday resort because of the large number of visitors who used to stay in furnished rooms not for one or two weeks but for several months.

One other thing we had to offer the visitors in those far-off days before the First World War was live entertainment. The Pavilion had live shows throughout the year and there were annual pierrot shows on the foreshore during the summers. There are no 'live' shows here now in summer or winter despite our 26,000-plus potential clientele.

24 December 1970

Staff at Beach Road School, around the 1930s.

An official guide of Cleveleys from the 1930s.

American Millionaire's Thornton Connections

Probably the most famous of all nineteenth-century American millionaires was Andrew Carnegie, born of God-fearing Scottish parents and a man who, throughout his life, believed that heaven helps those who help themselves. He was a fanatical believer in what Samuel Smiles, the famous Victorian, called 'self help' and the best way one could help oneself, according to the philosophy of Andrew Carnegie, was by improving oneself or, to be more specific, by knowing more.

Andrew Carnegie amassed heaven knows how many millions – I doubt whether he himself knew how many millions he was worth – from his iron and steel works in the United States, but what distinguished him from other millionaires of his time was that he gave astronomical sums away, chiefly by means of benefactions to libraries. The main free library in Blackpool, in Queen Street, is officially the Carnegie library, though nobody ever refers to it as such, but old Andrew's name is engraved over the main entrance in stone.

Ah yes, and there was another characteristic of Andrew Carnegie's which mustn't be forgotten: he was a Methodist and a half, a dyed-in-the-wool Nonconformist if ever there was one, and it was in 1910 that he provided £200 towards the organ in Mrs Janet Wignall's handsome new church in Thornton, which opened in 1915.

Twenty years before, in the 1880s, a ship named the *Janet Wignall* foundered near Dumfries and all hands were lost. That ship's owner was John Wignall, and the Wignall Methodist church at Thornton is a memorial to him. Its full name is still the Wignall Memorial Methodist church. Mrs Janet Wignall, after whom the ship was named, presented the church to Thornton Methodists or, as they were then, Wesleyans, because she and her husband, a leading figure in the shipping industry at Fleetwood for many years, had lived at Thornton during the summer.

While Mr and Mrs Wignall lived at 'The Lawsons' they regularly attended the old whitewashed Wesleyan church – it looked more like a barn than a church – which was in Victoria Road East, Thornton, near the site of the present Wignall church. It had originally opened as a place of worship in 1812, making it the first Methodist chapel in the Fylde. That old chapel was demolished several years before 1905 when the present Wignall church was built. The organ that Andrew Carnegie defrayed half the cost of was a famous fixture at the church for many years.

The reason I know about it is largely because of what Mr William Lancaster, the organist at the church for over forty years, told me, and from what a former minister of the church, a famous character called the Revd G. E. Mitchell, told my father. William Lancaster's father lived on for several years after the death of his son and the old man, Richard Lancaster, another fanatical Methodist, built the house in which I live.

Apart from the Carnegie grant, the original organ at the Wignall church could, Mr William Lancaster once told me, be said to owe its installation to hundreds of packets of treacle toffee and home-made jams of various kinds. The reason was that choir members raised money towards their organ from a series of efforts in their own homes. The original choirmaster in 1905 was Mr Harry Gregson, who worked at the United Alkali Works, Burn Naze, and Miss E. Taylor, who became Mrs Bradshaw, played the harmonium before the organ was installed.

When, with Andrew Carnegie's £200 grant, there was sufficient money to buy an organ, a Mr Haile was so moved by the occasion that he burst into verse. Mr Haile lived at one of the shops in Victoria Road East near Alexandra Road. He was blind, wore blue glasses and felt his way along the pavements with a walking stick. His poem started:

> 'We're going to have a new organ as sure as I'm a man,
> A regular, gradely good'un, brand new, spick and span.'

Later, after explaining that the committee were in difficulty about enlisting an organ blower, the verses suggested they should get Marsh Mill at Thornton – then a working mill – transferred

The first Wesleyan chapel in Thornton.

to raise the necessary wind because, continued the canto, it belonged to Mr John Parkinson, another famous local Methodist and a pillar of the Wignall church.

When the day finally arrived for the consecration of the new organ a Mrs Pickles, of Hawthorne Road, Thornton, opened it with a gold key. She, I am told, was the chief soprano in the choir.

I am not certain when Mr William Lancaster became the church's organist but it was before the First World War, and many were the stories he delighted in telling – and he was a splendid raconteur – of various men and boys who blew the organ bellows before an electricity supply was installed here in 1927. Mr Lancaster told me that there always seemed to be a wheezing gasp from the organ – signifying that the bellows had expired for lack of wind – when the organ was in full blast with something like 'Bread of Heaven', a hymn which is almost a trademark of Methodism.

After the installation of an electrical supply and the reconstruction of the organ to provide the church with its Mark II instrument, it was decided to move the organ from the loft above the choir stalls to a ledge above the entrance porch, with the console in the front pew. That didn't last very long, however, according to what Mr William Lancaster told me, because the folk in the back pews soon learned things about the church organ they had never previously suspected. It was like sitting in an organ chamber and there were sighs and squeaks, groans, grunts and moans to say nothing of the sudden fortissimos that nearly lifted the worshippers out of their seats.

Mr Lancaster, Mr Willie Lancaster as many people called him, delighted in telling of these incidents and, according to him, either the organ had to be moved or there would be a reduction in the number of worshippers at the Wignall Methodist church. I well recall Mr Lancaster with a Buster Keaton expressionless face saying 'one of them had to go,' and it was, of course, the organ. The works were put back again in the old organ loft and everyone seemed happy once again.

Both my parents admired the preaching of the Revd G. E. Mitchell, whom I mentioned earlier in this article, and I remember him very well. Of only two ministers I have known could it be said that they regularly had their congregations roaring with laughter and both of them had more that a touch of Charlie Chaplin in them. One was Mr Mitchell, who looked rather like George Robey, and who had an irrepressible sense of fun both in and out of the pulpit, and the other, of course, was the Revd W.T. Evans, the Vicar of Layton for many years. They were two real characters.

22 January 1971

The new and old Wesleyan churches, Thornton.

The level-crossing at Burn Naze.

Burn Naze

Looking back over the astonishing growth and development of our district from its truly rural days, one comes upon certain milestones that arouse speculations. Examples of where a contrary turn of the wheel of fate would have made an enormous difference to the future include the siting of the tramway through the centre of Cleveleys instead of keeping it along the promenade, and the dropping of a plan for the railway station at Cleveleys.

The branch railway line from Preston to Fleetwood opened in 1840 and the railway station at Thornton was opened in 1870 with the Burn Naze station opening in 1903, the year the Wright brothers successfully flew a heavier than air machine for the first time and the year in which a then new invention was the principal talking point among men: the safety razor as patented by a man named King Gillette.

The railway station at Thornton, alas, closed down last year and however uneconomic it may have been I shall continue to regret its closure because of the part the railway station played in my life.

The project of a railway station at Cleveleys was first discussed after the First World War and it was decided to have a branch line from a point near Tarn Gate crossing at Thornton. A rough bridge was made over the dyke there in preparation for launching the scheme which would have resulted in one or two more level crossings here and, probably, the retention of the old railway station at Thornton, which before 1927, was on the south side of the level crossing in Victoria Road East. With a railway station at Cleveleys, there would have been no need for the station built in 1927 at Thornton. That station, the one that is to be seen now, was built a few years after the plans for a station at Cleveleys was dropped. The plans were dropped, as far as I know, for economic reasons.

With holiday traffic for Cleveleys by-passing Thornton, the influence on the seaside end of this district, as far as development in the 1920s was concerned, would have been enormous. Whether Cleveleys lost as much as some people thought at the time by the Lancashire and Yorkshire Railway Company having to abandon its plans is a matter that, in my younger days, provided plenty of material for debate and argument.

To switch to the other end of our district, the decision of the old United Alkali Company to open a soda ash works at Burn Naze was a move that had an enormous effect on the development of the whole of this district. It introduced new life and vigour into a rural village with fewer than 1,000 inhabitants, mostly farmers and their families. The United Alkali Works was built there with two huge chimneys dominating the site.

One man who could recall those days had substantial claims to be regarded as the best-known man in Thornton Cleveleys. He was Mr Jack Ashton, the postmaster at Thornton for heaven knows how many years. He died in the 1950s and the last time I met him was at his home in Woodland Avenue, Thornton, on his ninetieth birthday and at that age he was a regular cyclist. He cycled to see his married daughter at Stanah Gardens, Thornton, at least once a week and I remember Jack Ashton telling me on his ninetieth birthday that his mother lived to be ninety and his grandmother lived to be ninety-nine.

Jack Ashton was a wonderful old man and some of his earliest Thornton memories were of 'half-timing' when he attended Baines' Endowed School in the mornings and worked on a farm in the afternoons. He told me he vividly remembered walking to Singleton with his brother when he was a boy of seven or eight years of age to deliver a parcel, and when I asked him how he found his way there he told me that his mother had told him to follow the telegraph poles until he reached Little Singleton and then to make for the church. He left school at the age of twelve, worked as a shoemaker in Thornton for a few years and it was either in the late 1880s or nearly 1890s that he became Thornton's first full-time postmaster.

Jack Ashton knew Burn Naze before the Alkali Works as it was called – or the 'Chemic' – arrived there. Another Thornton old-timer I knew who remembered Burn Naze before the 'Chemic' was William Cartmell, who farmed Norcross for many years and who was born at Stanah. He died during the last war in his late eighties.

A curious thing about Burn Naze is that it was preserved as a rural retreat until so near the end of Queen Victoria's reign, for a decision had been made sixteen years previously which was to have altered Burn Naze completely. This was when the man who became Sir Peter Hesketh Fleetwood was planning his new port at the mouth of the River Wyre – New Liverpool, as at one time it was believed it would be named. He decided that the farmland known as Burn Naze should become the manufacturing district of his new town. Wyreton was the name finally chosen for the area and a pier and twenty cottages for workmen were planned.

Somewhere on the site a foundation stone was laid with traditional ceremonial, and speeches expressed unlimited confidence in the future of Wyreton. Unfortunately, when the job of building Fleetwood followed it cost so much money that Sir Peter's fortune dwindled rapidly and he had to sell his home, Rossall Hall, and leave for the South of England. That killed any hopes of Wyreton materializing and the peace and quiet of Burn Naze were to remain undisturbed – apart from the passing trains after 1840 – until the United Alkali works arrived there in the 1890s.

William Cartmell told me that he had caught pheasants and hares around Burn Naze. There was plenty of game around what are now the 'Corvic,' 'Darvic' and other huge ICI plants that looked liked something out of a science fiction film. Yes, there were hares and pheasants in what is now Burn Naze and William Cartmell often went hunting there when he was a young man. Or was it poaching?

26 March 1971

63

Local Link with the Viceroy's Palace

It must be something like fourteen or fifteen years ago that a sumptuous memorial volume was published about one of the greatest architects in this country, Sir Edwin Lutyens, and I suppose most architects would regard him as the greatest British architect of the twentieth century. He designed the magnificent Viceroy's Palace at Delhi, and also the Menin Gate, near Ypres, that once-seen-never-forgotten memorial to the men of the British and British Empire armies who were killed in the First World War. I saw the Menin Gate in 1929 when I was one of a party from Baines Grammar School, Poulton-le-Fylde, who went on a fortnight's holiday at Heyst on the Belgian coast.

In charge of the party were two masters from the school, Mr G. Rawes, then my form master, and Mr Harris, the French master. That was the first time I had ever been abroad and many things about that holiday I have long since forgotten. I have even forgotten what currency was in use then but I remember the Hindenburg Line extending across Belgium from the German border to the North Sea, I remember seeing workmen in Sanctuary Wood where, we were told, bodies were still being brought out for burial, I remember the ice creams of a man in Heyst promenade called Monsieur Lyons, and I remember forgetting about ice creams when I gazed on the thousands and thousands of names cut in the stone on the Menin Gate. It is now forty-two years since I, a schoolboy, saw the Menin Gate, but I doubt whether I shall ever forget it.

Architecturally speaking, it would seem that Sir Edwin Lutyens speciality was for grandiose buildings, including country houses, all of which were remarkable for their boldness of design, and Sir Edwin Lutyens was probably the only twentieth-century British architect who would have been capable of designing Buckingham Palace, Blenheim Palace or Welbeck Abbey.

Before he became internationally famous in the 1920s, he was, as it were, 'just another architect', but I wonder how many people know that, as a young architect, he designed houses in Thornton Cleveleys? His houses, still to be seen, were built soon after the turn of the century at Rossall Beach and a few years before the 1906 Cleveleys Cottage Exhibition which, more that anything else, put Cleveleys on the map.

Rossall Beach in 1906 had its own sea wall, described at the time as 'one of the cheapest sea defence works constructed on the coast of the British Isles, and one of the most effective. The face of the wall is concave, with an upper formation known as "bull-nose"; the powerful waves of the Irish Sea in times of storm strike the wall, are thrown back upon themselves, and so dissipate their energy harmlessly.'

That prose masterpiece comes from the official catalogue of the Cleveleys Cottage Exhibition of 1906, held soon after building had started at the Rossall Beach estate, and I suppose I must be one of the few people to have a copy of that catalogue.

The passage about the effectiveness of the sea-wall at Rossall Beach is not to be taken too seriously. Those who remember the bull-nose wall there will recall that it was not very high and every time there was a high tide whipped up by a strong wind the sea poured over the bull-nose wall and flooded areas of Thornton Gate and Rossall Beach.

It was in 1905, the year of a sweeping victory for the Liberals, headed by Campbell-Bannerman, in the general election, that a house was built in Church Road, Thornton, which was a good example of attractive building allied with cheapness, and it attracted hundreds of sightseers. It was soon after that all kinds of influential people, excited by the recent opening of Letchworth Garden City, decided to copy the idea at Cleveleys. The Lancashire and Yorkshire Railway Company, the Fleetwood Estate Company and local architects, chiefly Mr T.G. Lumb, who died in his nineties in 1953, and also Mr Bertram Drummond, wholeheartedly co-operated.

Oddly enough, the 1906 Cleveleys Cottage Exhibition, which proved a spectacular success, was not sponsored in any way by the local council nor in the official programme of the exhibition is there any mention of the council helping at all with the exhibition. The chairman of the exhibition's executive committee was Mr David Abercrombie of Manchester, and Mr

Lutyen's designer houses at Rossall Beach.

Lumb, a young architect and soon to be chairman of the Bispham and Norbreck Urban District Council, was a member, or to be more accurate, was a dozen members rolled into one.

The primary idea behind the exhibition was to invite architects and builders to 'have a go' at different styles of houses and prizes were offered in different classes to those architects and builders whose designs and buildings, in the opinion of the judges, offered the best value for money. The exhibition show houses are still to be seen in Stockdove Way, Whiteside Way and West Drive and the headquarters of the exhibition was what is now the West Drive Park Club at the junction of West Drive and Rossall Road.

Obviously, with hindsight, one would expect the prices of houses then to be far less than house prices today. Yes, but even so there are almost unlimited shocks in store for anyone browsing through the catalogue of the 1906 Cleveleys Cottage Exhibition. One's first reaction on reading specifications and prices is to wonder whether the official catalogue isn't liberally sprinkled with printer's errors. How about this to start with? A semi-detached house with three bedrooms and a boxroom – this would be four bedrooms by today's standards – a living room 13ft square cost ... well, go on, guess.

The freehold price, believe it or not, was £147 16s 5d. If this design was to be duplicated, however, it would cost more like £174 19s 5d. Could the fivepence in both figures, one wonders, be the builder's profit?

One of the showpieces of the exhibition was a beautifully designed detached house at the corner of West Drive and Cleveleys Avenue. This property, called 'the Dutch Cottage', won the premier award in its particular class.

Prizes awarded jointly to architects and builders were substantial. In two classes for instance, 'the best and most economical detached cottage with not less than three bedrooms', and 'the best and most economical pair of cottages, with not less than three bedrooms each', there were first prizes for £100 each which, I suppose, represents well over £10,000 by today's values. Altogether, the prize money totalled £396.

Local rates, by the way, were then 5s 11d in the pound, of which 11d was for Poor Law purposes, 1s 9d was the Lancashire County Council's precept and 3s 3d was for the local 'kitty'. In the following year, 1907, the local rates – take a deep breath and hold on to your back teeth – were reduced, yes reduced, to 5s 4d.

30 April 1971

65

Remarkable Repertoire of Ghost, Wreck and Prank

I wrote last week about Thornton Parish Council from 1894 to 1900 and I mentioned in those days local people could and sometimes did evade paying rates. Farmers – and there was hardly anybody else living here in those days except farmers – used to carry shale and gravel from the beach for making or repairing roads and footpaths. The old parish council paid 7s a day for horse, cart and carter, and one could pay one's rates in this way. Some people did.

I suppose there must still be a few people around who can recall the days of Thornton Parish Council, which ceased seventy-one years ago, and I knew several people who recalled those days. One was William Betney, a famous local character and a member of the old parish council, whose council career extended into the 1930s. Another was Cllr William Cartmel, who was born at Stanah in the 1850s and who died during the last war, and another was Mr John Barnes, of Cleveleys, about whom I wrote two articles recently. Finally and, to complete the list as far as I am concerned, there was Mr Robert Hindle, a licensee of the Cleveleys Hotel for many years, who was elected to the new Thornton Urban District Council in 1900, and there was Mr Richard Southworth.

Mr Southworth, of Fleetwood Road, Thornton, died about fifteen years ago and he could vividly recall the wreck of the *Abana*, a Norwegian ship which was wrecked off Little Bispham and the remains of which can still be clearly seen at low tide. When he was a boy, Richard Southworth worked as a carter shifting sand and gravel from Cleveleys beach and he could remember when a ship called *Pride of the Weaver* brought stones for local roads to Victoria Dock, which was a landing area near what is now called Stanah Clough. This is now the site of a slade which is extensively used in summer for dinghies and water skiers at Stanah and is on the edge of the car park.

The old bone mill at Skippool, near what is now the headquarters of the Blackpool and Fleetwood Yacht Club, was then in use and boats used to carry bones and bone meal from the mill. The old mill was demolished in the 1930s.

Richard Southworth, a grand old character with a truly remarkable memory, once recalled

Abana wrecked at Little Bispham.

The Thornton Gala, 1910.

for me one black stormy night in December 1894 when the *Abana* was wrecked. He was a lad of, I think, twelve years of age at the time and his uncle and somebody else bought the wreck after the ship breaker had finished with it. Richard helped to cart timber from the wreck to a timber yard at Marton. 'There was plenty of good timber on the *Abana*,' Richard Southworth told me.

The crew were rescued by the Blackpool lifeboat which had had to travel from Central Beach – the lifeboat house site at Blackpool hasn't changed – but because there was no coast road then, it had to be pulled by horses from the Gynn along what is now Devonshire road and through Bispham village until it arrived just north of Norbreck.

Richard Southworth was born in Fleetwood Road, Thornton, opposite what is now the Employment Exchange and later he went to live near Four Lane Ends. It was whilst he was living near Four Lane Ends that he encountered his first – and his last – 'ghost'. It must be now nearly twenty years since I heard him tell this story but the memory of it is as vivid to me now as it was then. Richard Southworth had been playing cards at Carter's Club near Thornton railway station and he got home late. He had just closed the cottage door when he heard a clanking noise outside. He looked out but could see nothing, but as soon as he went indoors again the clanking started again. Richard Southworth didn't know what to do but he admitted he thought about ghosts. He went to bed. A few days afterwards he discovered that one of his cats had got caught in a rat trap and had dragged it around the yard trying to free itself.

Richard Southworth won first prize for the best kept horse in the first civic procession ever to be held in Thornton Cleveleys and that was in 1897 to celebrate Queen Victoria's Diamond Jubilee. I remember being surprised that he could remember so well and he told me that there were twenty or thirty decorated carts in the procession.

Richard Southworth could recall an enormous number of early gala days. He recalled one where Billy Hardman, brother of George Hardman, the famous Church Road primary school headmaster for so many years, organized a field day in a field opposite the Windmill. This is now the site of Marsh Neys Estate.

Richard Southworth also recalled for me the days when Thornton had eleven 'devils'. These

Thornton Gala at Bay House, 1910.

were eleven farm lads who used to gather in the kitchen of Nook House Farm – and confirmation classes were held there too, old Richard told me. These eleven lads were always up to some mischief. I asked him what he meant, and he recalled one of the pranks.

The eleven 'devils', or some of them, decided to put an end to a dance at Tom Smith's farm loft in Marsh Road, Thornton. Everything was going well at the dance when things started to go wrong. People began coughing and spluttering and the dancers tried to open the trap door and windows but these were all locked. Finally, someone smashed a window to get some fresh air.

What had happened was that someone had put cayenne pepper in a bundle of hay and lit a fire under it, sending fumes up into the loft where the dance was taking place. I remember saying something like, 'It might have been worse,' when old Richard produced his 'punch line'. There was a couple of hundredweight of gunpowder stored in the same building, he told me.

There were many stories around in his young days about a ghost at Bourne Hall, he told me. He had heard that this ghost used to milk the cows and sweep out the shippons before the farmer got up. Everyone talked about the Bourne Hall ghost, said Richard, but he never saw it – and he tried often enough as a lad.

Richard Southworth recalled working as a beater for grouse and pheasants when there were shoots at The Towers, off Holmefield Avenue. The gamekeeper there was a famous local character called Kess Hodgkinson and John Barnes, as a young man, had worked there in the days when The Towers estates stretched to what is now Burn Naze and included Pheasant Wood – the name was no accident – Woodcock Wood and many other copses and woods that have long, long disappeared. Richard Southworth could remember the days when Mr T.G. Lumb lived at The Towers and sixty or seventy brace of pheasants were shot in one afternoon.

I asked him why this game area didn't continue longer and I shall always remember his reply. No, that's not right. I shall always remember his facial expression when he replied, 'Well, you see, there was so much poaching going on all the time.' I don't want to be unjust to the fellow, but I thought then and I think now, twenty years later, that he knew more about this poaching epidemic at The Towers than he admitted. I'm sure of it.

4 June 1971

A Piece of History Sold on the Cheap

Tempus fugit – not 'arf, it doesn't – and however hard I try and deny it, nothing can alter the fact that it is nearly twenty years since I went to the Regal Hotel, Cleveleys, where Mr Sidney Goodall, a local estate agent, offered for sale the biggest piece of history in Thornton Cleveleys – Marsh Mill, built in 1794 – and nobody wanted it. The first bid was £1,500 and the second was £2,000. The third and final bid was £2,250 and Mr Goodall, try as he would, couldn't get another shilling out of his audience.

The sale, I think, had been widely publicized, and the historic importance of Thornton's Marsh Mill had been emphasized, but almost nobody was interested in acquiring a piece of eighteenth-century history at a giveaway price. The property was, of course, withdrawn, and it was eventually acquired by the local council to whom it has belonged ever since.

Marsh Mill had previously been on the market on the 1930s. It had been a café and it was the scene of a tragedy during those days when two women fell to their deaths from the outside platform on the first storey. Afterwards it was vacant and after the last war it became, for several years, a warehouse for a firm making plastic products not far away in Occupation Road.

In the 1930s when the future of the mill was in doubt, a public meeting was called to find if anything could be done to preserve it. Some people thought at the time that it might be demolished. One of the staunchest supporters of the move to urge the council to buy the mill was Mr J. Murgatroyd, of Rossendale Avenue South, a queer old bearded character who lived with his sister in a house crammed with masses of bric-à-brac. How real was the threat to demolish the mill in the 1930s? I don't know, but it was saved by the Merrill family of Thornton then who gave it a new coat of white paint and made essential repairs to the structure of the building.

To local people Marsh Mill is such a familiar landmark that we tend to take it for granted. That's why it is always pleasing to hear visitors praise the landmark because their comments remind us what an attractive local feature Marsh Mill is.

Some of us can remember the scene before the mill went into permanent retirement shortly after the First World War. Though only a child, I can remember it as a working mill and what a delight it was to watch the huge sails revolving creakily in the wind while below in the adjoining smithy came the ringing of the blacksmith's anvil. That smithy continued working long, long after the last bag of corn was ground by Marsh Mill.

The mill yard was the real community centre of Thornton in the old days. Wagons stacked with grain arrived there and the pile of bulging sacks of flour got higher and higher inside the mill.

The horse was still lord of the land then and powerful, handsome shire horses clip-clopped into the mill yard daily because all local farms relied on the smithy then for shoeing their horses. The blacksmith I remember was called Mr Simmonds and he came from Poulton-le-Fylde daily in a pony cart. Like other people of their generation, my parents were both keen on walking – in my boyhood days people liked walking for walking's sake irrespective of their social standing. I think they particularly enjoyed walking to or past Marsh Mill. Their young son certainly did, though he was always reluctant to walk past the mill despite the fact that tea and cakes awaited him from Miss Pilkington at Villamar, a house that then included all the land now occupied by the county library, Lecture Hall and Lecture Hall car park. Some of my earliest and happiest memories are of Marsh Mill with its huge sails revolving and its machinery creaking away inside those stout, whitewashed walls.

Marsh Mill was built in 1794, five years after the start of the French Revolution, at the time of the 'Terror' in France when Maximilien Robespierre was 'gaffer' and heads – and not always aristocrats' heads – rolled from the guillotine daily. It was built by Ralph Slater, a famous builder of windmills in the Fylde for the Hesketh family of Rossall Hall, and it was built five years before the passing of the Thornton Marsh Act of 1799.

The landscape over which Marsh Mill originally presided had a much more desolate

The Old Windmill

A Fylde Landmark.

BUILT in 1794, this mill has been the outstanding feature of the Fylde, it contains some Wonderful Wooden Machinery, which can be viewed together with the fine country round on payment of a small fee. :: The first two floors have been converted into a CAFE and, as these specimen menus will show, visitors can spend a pleasant hour at the Windmill, Thornton.

1/- Windmill Teas

Pot of Tea, Bread and Butter, Jam, Piece of Cake.

1/6 TEA

Pot of Tea, Bread and Butter, Fruit and Cream.

Ham and Egg, Pot of Tea Bread and Butter - 2/-

Sweets, Chocolates, Mineral Waters and Novelties.

Rooms let for Picnic, Wedding and other Parties. Parking Ground for Patrons' Cars and Char-a-bancs.

Advertisement for the Old Windmill.

appearance then when the Marsh Act brought hedges for the enclosures, roads, sea defences and more adequate dykes for drainage. The workmen building the mill must have looked out over an expanse of marsh which, if it resembled anything today, would be not dissimilar to Pilling Sands.

During its declining years in the 1928s and 1930s Marsh Mill endured many slights and indignities. Previously it had had a road named after it, Mill Lane, but local councillors decided in the 1920s that this name wasn't 'posh' enough, so it was changed to Woodland Avenue. After years of being unwanted, however, Marsh Mill partly came into its own again in 1950 when Thornton Cleveleys celebrated its fiftieth anniversary as an urban district council. A remarkable exhibition was held at Thornton Lecture Hall to commemorate the event and a local man, Mr Ellis Tomlinson, then a master at Baines' Grammar School, Poulton-le-Fylde, the school he attended as a boy, devised armorial bearings for Thornton Cleveleys. Mr Tomlinson, a Thornton resident, was then acknowledged as a leading authority on matters heraldic and his coat of arms for Thornton Cleveleys has Marsh Mill as its most prominent feature. Until 1950 Thornton Cleveleys didn't have an official coat of arms at all and Mr Tomlinson, who formerly lived with his mother and father in Fleetwood Road North, Thornton, not far from Marsh Mill, restored this grand old building to its rightful place on our civic coat of arms.

Believe it or not, there was a time soon after the turn of the century – let the dreadful truth be told – when some local councillors anxious that this district should have an official coat of arms, suggested that it incorporate the three chimneys of the then United Alkali Company at Burn Naze, which after 1926, became the ICI.

2 July 1971

The oldest local school in Thornton, Baines Endowed School.

Ten Shillings for the Annual Dinner

The former headmaster of Baines' Grammar School, Poulton-le-Fylde, Mr F.J. Stafford, didn't have much of a retirement. He was headmaster of the school from the early 1920s until he retired in 1953 and he then left Poulton-le-Fylde and moved to Whiteside Way, Cleveleys – he lived exactly at the rear of my house – and he died after a retirement of only a year.

He was my headmaster from 1926 until 1930 and while I was at his school, I was friendly with his only son, Frank, who died when he was thirteen or fourteen, and, together with scores of pupils at the school, I attended his funeral. I doubt Mr Stafford ever completely recovered from that blow.

Baines' Grammar School at Poulton-le-Fylde and Baines' Endowed School at Thornton were both founded in the eighteenth century and they are named after a Poulton draper, Mr James Baines, who died in 1717. Mr Baines left the schoolhouse which had been erected for him on Thornton Marsh to Peter Woodhouse of Thornton – Woodhouse Road at Thornton is named after the family – together with six other men, and according to Mr Baines' will the school was to be used for ever as a free school for Thornton boys and girls.

He also left to his trustees twenty-one acres of land at Carleton with the proviso that the rent from this land – less ten shillings a year which had to be deducted annually to defray the cost of a dinner for the school's trustees – was to pay for the services of a suitable headmaster.

By the early nineteenth century, a Mr Simpson of Thornton, left an endowment of £500 towards the cost and maintenance of this school. A new structure was then built on the original site of the old building and a public subscription fund was launched which resulted in £100 being raised.

The schoolmaster was elected and, where necessary, was dismissed by the trustees of the school – there is no record so far as I know, of any headmaster being sacked – and the trustees waived their annual claim to the ten shillings Mr Baines had left for their annual beano.

Although the ten bob would not go far today – I suppose it could be stretched to defray the cost of baked beans on toast for the favoured few at the top table – it would have been enough even for the gargantuan appetite of our forefathers who were, at that time, still talking about Queen Victoria's recent marriage to the young Prince Albert of Saxe-Coburg. In 1846 best beef cost 6d a pound, potatoes were 1s 10d for 20lb, fresh salmon was 10d a pound and fresh eggs were 1s for eighteen at Fleetwood Market.

Mr Baines was a great believer in the value of education – eighteenth-century pamphleteers and authors all seemed to regard education as a panacea for all mankind's ills – and shortly before his death, James Baines had another school built near Poulton-le-Fylde, at a place called Hardhorn. In his will, he left this to various of his yeomen and gentlemen friends, 'to remain, continue and to be a free school for ever for the persons and purposes hereinafter named.'

There were seven trustees appointed and they too were entitled under the conditions of the will to an annual ten-bob dinner 'and after all costs for repairs at the said schoolhouse and grounds it stands on be paid, the balance be given to such persons as shall yearly and every year be named, chosen, and appointed by the seven said trustees, and their successors, or the major part of them, to act as schoolmaster, to teach and instruct in writing, reading and other school learning, according to the best of his capacity, all such children of the inhabitants of the townships of Poulton and Hardhorn-in-Newton as shall be sent to the said school.' The pupils were to 'behave themselves with good manners' and the master had no other payment or reward 'except what the said children or their parents shall voluntarily give.'

Like Thornton School, the trustees were empowered to sack a headmaster not up to his job. His hours of duty were from 7 a.m. till 11 a.m. and from 1 p.m. to 5 p.m. except for 1 November to 1 February, in which quarter the hours were from 8 a.m. to 11 a.m. and 1 p.m. to 4 p.m., 'the afternoons of Thursday and Saturday to be a holiday'. Mr Baines also left £800 for the poorest

Thornton church.

Mr Jagger's class at the Baines Endowed School.

inhabitants of Marton, Hardhorn, Carleton and Thornton.

Thornton Cleveleys, of course, has had a strong link with Baines' Endowed School, Thornton, and with Baines' Grammar School, Poulton-le-Fylde, since the eighteenth century, and this district also has very close links with Rossall School.

It was in 1843 that a group of local gentlemen – that was the word used – studied the possibilities of a Church of England school at Rossall, until then the home of Sir Peter Hesketh Fleetwood, Lord of the Manor, after whom the town at the mouth of the River Wyre is named. The keenest of the men urging such a school for the education of clergymen's sons and other 'gentlemen' – that word is never far away – was the Revd St Vincent Beechey, who from 1841 to 1846 was vicar at Thornton parish church, which had been opened in 1835. A committee was elected to study the scheme and Mr Beechey was elected secretary.

On 22 August 1844 the Northern Church of England School at Rossall was opened with forty pupils and the Revd John Woolley was the first headmaster. After only one term, however, there were 115 boys at the school, which continued to be called the Northern Church of England School until 1870 when it was renamed Rossall School. The Revd St Vincent Beechey remained secretary to the school governors from its opening until he left Thornton in 1846.

Links between Thornton and Rossall School have remained strong: Mr R.K. Melluish was a master at the school for very many years and a Diocesan reader at Thornton parish church. The Revd C.E. Young AFC JP, a former headmaster of Rossall School, frequently conducted services at Thornton parish church; his school secretary, Miss Gloria Tomlinson – later Mrs Reay – was assistant organist at the church and the organist was Mr G.F. Suart, a master at Rossall School. After Mr Young left Rossall School and moved to Keswick, Mr G.S. Sale, Rossall School's new headmaster, maintained the strong links between Rossall and Thornton parish church.

Here is a delightful and true story about Mr Young's days as headmaster at Rossall. He was, as everyone who knew him even slightly was well aware, a scholarly, quiet man who, in my opinion, had lost the common touch. He had a marvellous ability whenever he addressed a public meeting and he was in great demand locally as a speaker.

On one occasion in winter he had been addressing members of the Mount Road Men's Fellowship at Fleetwood and for some reason or other his car was off the road. Mr Young politely declined a lift back to Rossall School and after a chat with various people he started to walk back to Rossall and, as it was late, he walked along the tram track from Ash Street to Rossall. It was cold, it was windy and it started to rain when a late staff car went by on its final journey to the Bispham depot. The tram driver saw the young man walking along and took pity on him. 'Cleveleys? Norbreck? Bispham?' he shouted to Mr Young after opening the window in his driver's compartment. 'Yes, keep straight on,' said Mr Young, deep in thought as usual. That story was told me by a master as Rossall.

Occasionally absent-minded Mr Young might had been, but I wish there were more people in the world like him.

6 August 1971

Cleveleys Used to be Called Lower Thornton

In 1906, the year of the spectacularly successful Cleveleys Cottage Exhibition which represented the origin of modern Cleveleys, nine local people decided to subscribe £10 each into a fund with which to start a mission church at Cleveleys. This mission church became known as the 'Institute' and was the forerunner of St Andrew's parish church which was dedicated in 1910.

One of the nine people who helped to finance the mission church was a local plumber, Mr John Whitby, who came to Cleveleys in the 1880s from Liverpool where he was born. John Whitby died in his mid-eighties and he had an almost inexhaustible fund of stories about Thornton Cleveleys in the good or bad old days. John Whitby came to Cleveleys to work for a famous local landowner, Major W. Nutter, after whom Nutter Road is named. Major Nutter had a bungalow on the north side of what is now Victoria Road West, but was then called Ramper Road, and he also had a boathouse. John Whitby started work here on extensions to Cleveleys Hotel in the days when beer was threehalfpence a gill and public houses were open from eight in the morning until ten or eleven at night. Those days continued until the outbreak of war in 1914.

In the 1880s when John Whitby came to Cleveleys there was, officially, no Cleveleys. The place was referred to as 'Lower Thornton'. Ramper Road, or Victoria Road as it is now, was surrounded by open fields and farmland and John Whitby recalled when this area was teeming with rabbits. The land was known as the rabbit warrens, he told me, and Major Nutter used to spend hours shooting them. The rabbit warrens are now, of course, the site of supermarkets, car parks and shops.

Oddly enough, despite the fact that Cleveleys, sorry Lower Thornton, had nothing to offer the visitor except an unlimited number of rabbits and huge stretches of unspoilt sandhills, there were plenty of visitors during the summer, according to John Whitby. They were, however, not the type of visitor who wants self-service flats. According to John Whitby most of them brought their own servants with them and they stayed at the Cleveleys Hydro or took over houses, not for a week or a fortnight but for at least a month. The reason they came here, according to John Whitby, was because of the bracing air, the sea, and the fact that Cleveleys was undeveloped.

There used to be a single troupe of pierrots who, after changing their costumes behind the old Cleveleys Inn on what is now called North Promenade, performed on the beach. When not on the beach they trundled their little harmonium to the front of the inn and, as soon as they had amassed enough money to cover the price of a drink, they tossed to decide who should have the drink.

Those were the days when as a modern communiqué might say communications were difficult. Difficult, but they did exist. There were the wagonettes which plied between Blackpool and Cleveleys Hotel, returning to Blackpool via Castle Gardens at Carleton. The cabbies who jogged along between Cleveleys and Thornton railway station with their fares cursed heartily later on when Mr Parker of Rossall Beach bought two early motor buses and ran these over the same route at threepence per person per trip.

Thornton Cleveleys, needless to say, abounded in characters in John Whitby's early days here. I remember him telling me about the old postman from Poulton who rode in a red governess cart and wore blue spectacles and as he walked from cottage to cottage the pony followed him without him giving it any orders. There was Bobby Cragg, the one and only representative of the law in Thornton Cleveleys. He had an old dog which followed him wherever he went but it was a peaceful community and there was never any need to lock anyone up in the little old police station which was a cottage in Rossall Road near what is now Victoria Square. The only prevalent crime in those days was drunkenness and this was fairly widespread, but 'the law' left the topers to sleep it off provided, of course, they didn't make a nuisance of themselves and, according to John Whitby, they hardly ever did.

Whitby's plumber and painter's house, Victoria Road, Cleveleys.

Mr Whitby was on friendly terms with a well-known character, Mr Kewley, who lived in a whitewashed cottage where is now the entrance to Anchorsholme Park near Anchorsholme crossing, and Mr Kewley used to regulate the trams – the tramroad system was built in 1896 – with red and green flags.

I started by telling of Mr Whitby's connection with the old Institute, the forerunners of St Andrew's parish church, and there can't be many people who remember it when it was the church. I remember it well enough but not when it was a church. It was later used as a hall and Sunday school before the Memorial Hall – to commemorate the men of St Andrew's who were killed in the First World War – was opened in 1926.

In winter, when snow made walking difficult, Mr Whitby would clear a path from the mission church or Institute to the tram station and along that path he fixed temporary posts and oil storm-lamps. I knew him well in his old age and he was a grand old man, a real link with rural days. How he would have relished the exhibition that was staged at St Andrew's church last year to celebrate the church's sixtieth anniversary.

15 October 1971

The Day the Library Came to Town

Just twenty years ago, at the end of October 1951, the Holme Moss television transmitter was opened and television became the latest novelty and talking point in this part of the country. I am, I think, correct in saying that all television sets were nine-inch models, the same as the original television sets which a few Londoners had in the late 1930s when television broadcasts started from Alexandra Palace.

It was in 1938, the year of Munich and the year in which the British people were issued with respirators, and I spent a few days with a friend of mine who lived at Maida Vale, London, and he and I visited a nearby friend of his one evening and there on the table I saw something I had never seen before: a television set, a working television set. It was a nine-inch model and I gazed open-mouthed at this scientific miracle – every square inch of it – and though I can't remember what programme I saw I wonder how many people now can say they saw a working television set in the 1930s?

This, though I never suspected it at the time, was the start of a major social revolution and it is now becoming increasingly difficult to remember how people spent their leisure hours before, just twenty years ago, television arrived in this part of the world. What did people do with their spare time before 1951? (Or rather before 1952, because that was the year when television sets really began to sell in earnest.) People went to the cinema, sometimes several times weekly, they listened to the radio, and they read books.

Talking of books and reading reminds me that it was forty years ago this year that the small Cleveleys branch of the county library in West Drive West opened with Miss Edith Ashworth as librarian. The splendid library at Four Lane Ends, Thornton, wasn't opened until seven years later, in 1938, and Thornton readers before that used to borrow books from a room at the Council Offices.

Miss Edith Ashworth.

Miss Edith Ashworth.

Those early days were hectic ones for Miss Ashworth and there were regularly queues of people entering the library to change their books or to join the service and, at the same time, there was another queue of people waiting to have their books stamped before they left. I hadn't long left school and I must have been one of the first borrowers from the then new Cleveleys library. Believe it or not, that library was always busy then and many people were avid readers in those days and books were a popular topic of conversation. What did people read? Some read, as now, books on tomato culture, motor car maintenance and so on, others read books about history, theology, literature and similar subjects but most people were insatiable readers of fiction, including the perennially popular 'westerns'.

Sapper was one of the most popular and prolific authors of the 1920s with his novels and *Bulldog Drummond* stories, and so was Dornford Yates and a host of others, and it was about this time that detective stories began their era of mass popularity with authors like Dorothy Sayers, S.S. Van Dine, J.J. Connington and countless others. For some reason that I think has never been made clear, there was an enormous spate of books about the First World War in the late 1920s and early 1930s.

There had been war books published during the 1920s – I am thinking of R.H. Mottram's *Spanish Farm* trilogy, Edmund Blunden's *Undertones of War* and a few others – but despite being well reviewed they never became anything remotely like best-sellers. It was in 1929 that the English version of Erich Maria Remarque's *All Quiet on the Western Front* appeared and this book caused a furore. It became a best-seller almost overnight and rapidly sold over a million copies. Forty years after its first appearance in English, it was reissued as a paperback. When I first joined the new Cleveleys branch of the county library, there was a long waiting list for *All Quiet* and for at least one more book, another best-seller but of a very different calibre: Dr Axel Munthe's *The Story of San Michele*. Until then, my recreational reading had consisted mainly of

The new library.

The Wide World magazine, Edgar Wallace, E. Phillips Oppenheim and an author now completely forgotten but popular then: William de Queux.

When the Cleveleys branch of the county library opened, among the first books I borrowed and read avidly – how odd that I should remember their titles after all these years – were *A Romanian Diary* by Hans Carossa, *A Fatalist at War* by Rudolph Binding, *The Case of Sargeant Grisha* by Arnold Zweig, *The Storm of Steel* by Ernst Junger and *War* by Ludwig Renn.

Whether coming events were casting their shadows I knew not then and I know not now, but ten years after this I had my own non-fictional baptism of fire. After reading as many war books as I could lay my hands on and after cross-examining various men who had fought in the First World War about these books' authenticity, I must have had a surfeit of blood and guts because I remember borrowing Dr Axel Munthe's best seller *The Story of San Michele*, a book I can still open anywhere and find as delightful as ever. I never thought, when I read those war books in my teens, that I would ever be involved at first-hand in warfare, but I was, and when I read Dr Axel Munthe I never thought I would ever see Anacapri in the Bay of Naples, but I did. I had my experience of war and my visit to Anacapri – it was an American officers' rest centre when I was there – as a result of accepting a shilling from His Majesty the late King George VI in early 1940.

To dear old Cleveleys Library I owe my early introduction to writers like Evelyn Waugh and Aldous Huxley and dozens, no, scores of other authors. The original Cleveleys library is still there, but the building is now used as a storeroom for the adjacent modern library, and to the old building, though derisorily small by modern standards, I owe an incalculable debt. Did any library anywhere have a more conscientious librarian than Miss Edith Ashworth who was Thornton Cleveleys' first librarian in 1931? I don't think so.

22 October 1971

The Story Behind some Local Road Names

When a road or avenue is completed, the normal procedure is for the builder to suggest a name which then goes before the local council for their approval. Usually this is a formality and only very infrequently is there any discussion about road names.

I well remember about eighteen or twenty years ago, however, when local councillors beamed with satisfaction when the name Winston Avenue was submitted. At the time Mr Churchill was Prime Minister, but several local names of roads, closely identified with some aspect of the neighbourhood in which they were set, have vanished as Thornton Cleveleys has developed.

It was just after the First World War that Mill Lane at Thornton had its name changed to Woodland Avenue. The reason for the change has never been clear to me despite the fact that I have enquired about the reasons for more years than I can remember. In the leafy days of fifty or sixty years ago I suppose there was some justification for changing a perfectly reasonable and very appropriate name like Mill Lane to Woodland Avenue because there were so many trees around Thornton's eighteenth-century Marsh Mill. Since the 1920s, however, so many trees have been cut down that the present name of the avenue has almost lost its significance.

There can't be many people around now who remember the origin of Nutter Road at Cleveleys. That name recalls a time when Major W. Nutter, of Accrington, was a famous local landowner and sportsman. He used a bungalow as a summer residence and he had a boathouse on the beach. What are now the sites of supermarkets and car parks were open fields in Major Nutter's days and the major apparently loved nothing better than organising 'shoots' all over

Major Nutter's bungalow, Cleveleys.

Nutter Road, Cleveleys, in the late 1920s.

the vast rabbit warrens that surrounded the cart track that was later to become Victoria Road West. Rabbits apparently swarmed in their thousands around Major Nutter's bungalow, according to what Mr John Whitby and Mr John Barnes told me many years ago.

Cleveleys was then little more than a few houses and farms behind miles of sandhills on which, in summer, bloomed endless clumps of sea-holly but nevertheless it was quite a famous little place before the First World War. The reason for its fame was that as many as 1,400 officers and men from East Lancashire towns camped at Cleveleys during the summer on and near the sandhills, and people came from Blackpool, Fleetwood and Poulton-le-Fylde with baskets of buns and cakes to sell to these soldiers. Even after the First World War, Cleveleys was popular as a summer camp for soldiers.

In the early 1920s when I attended the Beach Road Junior School – then called Beach Road Council School – hundreds of soldiers camped in tents on the surrounding fields and near what was Cullen's Camp, now the site of Cleveleys Men's Club in Slinger Road. We schoolboys stared in awe and wonder as men with one, two or three stripes on their jackets bawled and shouted at those who lacked these distinguishing marks. I can even recall after fifty years and more some of the forbidden words that were used by these men!

Long, long before Britain had khaki-clad soldiers and even before '1066 and all that', Holmes Road, Thornton, had an illustrious pedigree. Before the Normans there was a part of Thornton known as Holmes. It contained roughly that portion of rising ground stretching away from the Sacred Heart church towards Town End Farm – where Wordsworth Avenue and surrounding avenues are now. Holmes comes from an old Norse word and indicated a dry place in a morass. This land was surrounded by a dyke which flowed into the River Wyre but it had a habit of overflowing so that the lower-lying land was generally waterlogged, especially in winter.

Holmes Road used to be a delightfully winding country lane and I remember it in the 1920s for two chief reasons: the Lambert family lived there and they included two sons, identical twins, who were my contemporaries at school. Their home had a huge garden and not far from them was a semi-detached house with a workshop adjoining. This was the property of a jovial, red-cheeked little man named Thomas Eastham, a joiner.

Pool Foot Farm, near the Sacred Heart church, seems a very unusual name but this is a reminder of the days when land around there was often flooded.

It is easy to find out why many local roads and avenues are so named, but I wonder how many people know the origin of Gamble Road at Burn Naze, Thornton? Early in the nineteenth century Josiah Gamble, a chemical manufacturer, was one of the pioneers in the rapidly developing chemical industry and he went into partnership with a James Muspratt, another leading character in the chemical industry. Towards the end of the century another member of the Gamble family, Sir Christopher, comes on the scene. He was related to Josiah, but what the relationship was I don't know.

Bill Betney, who was a member of Thornton Parish Council from 1896 to 1900 and a member of Thornton Cleveleys Urban District Council from its origin in 1900 until the middle 1930s, once interviewed Sir Christopher. This happened in the early years of this century when Cllr Betney wanted to have a railway station at Burn Naze, principally because of the presence there of the United Alkali Works. This was a pet scheme of his for many years and it eventually triumphed and the station opened in 1906. Gamble Road is named after Sir Christopher Gamble. Alas, the railway station at Burn Naze is closed now but that's not the only thing around here that has changed in the last sixty years. Some things, however, haven't changed much.

Large areas of Thornton Cleveleys still suffer from flooding but this problem should be cured once and for all in the next few years. A pumping-station at the bottom of River Road, Thornton, already goes a long way to alleviating the problem of flooding in large areas on the eastern side of Thornton Cleveleys. This is a time of year when many people will be buying *The Guinness Book of Records* for somebody for Christmas and, for the record, that pumping station in River Road contains the largest Archimedes screw pumps in Britain.

23 December 1971

Palm Lounge, Cleveleys Hydro.

Luxury Tariff of Seven and Six

Just over sixty-four years ago, in December 1907, one of the biggest and best local hotels had its eastern wing added with forty bedrooms and a variety of remedial baths. That hotel was Cleveleys Hydro which was demolished in 1957 and which was originally Eringo Lodge, the home of Blackpool's first Mayor, Alderman John Cocker, in 1870. With interior decorations in what was called Art Nouveau style, all the ground floor of the new wing was occupied by dressing rooms and baths which offered Turkish, Russian, Aix-les-Bains, sitz, brine, sulphur and Nauheim treatments. These were the great days of hydros, short for hydropathic hotels, and Cleveleys Hydro had a national reputation until it closed in 1939.

During the last war it was part of the Ministry of Pensions, a hospital for RAF officers, a branch of the Ministry of the National Insurance and finally, before its demolition, a hostel for civil servants. The original Hydro building, minus the 1907 Italian wing, was a shooting lodge and just a century ago Alderman John Cocker had a fine herd of deer there which wandered on what was afterwards an eighteen-hole golf course.

Eringo Lodge afterwards came into the possession of a Mr Benjamin Sykes, of Poulton-le-Fylde, who altered the lodge into a 'hydropathic hotel' and it was opened to the public for the

84

first time in 1889. In 1904 a company with a capital of £55,000 took over the Hydro and the principal director was Mr James Richardson of Poulton-le-Fylde. Cleveleys Hydro then had 150 bedrooms and in the main hall lounge were two pedestals made out of the copper saved from Nelson's ship *Foudroyant*, which fought at Trafalgar and which met its end off Blackpool during a storm in the 1890s.

Several flower vases in the Hydro were also made from copper taken from the *Foudroyant* and, appropriately, there were statues of Nelson and Wellington in the main lounge. The main dining room accommodated 180 people, there was an organ for music recitals, a ballroom 100ft by 30ft with a sprung floor, and electric lift and the rooms and lounges were all lit by electricity.

In 1907, when the east wing was added, there was, of course, no electricity supply in this part of the world, but the Hydro generated its own supplies from a plant at the rear of the building alongside a garage which accommodated twenty cars. Also alongside the garage was another building, the stables for the horses and carriages. In 1907 a 14hp Napier bus and a horse-drawn landau met visitors who arrived at Thornton railway station to stay at Cleveleys Hydro.

In advertisements of the time, the prospective visitor is informed that Cleveleys Hydro can be reached by either Thornton railway station or via the two railway stations at Blackpool. If Blackpool Central station was used and visitors travelled from there to Cleveleys Hydro by tram, a change had to be made at the Gynn and passengers transferred to the Blackpool and Fleetwood Tramroad Company. There was a direct service to North Station, Blackpool, or Talbot Road as it was called.

Cleveleys Hydro, of course, was a luxury hotel and weekend visitors paid from 22s 6d from Friday breakfast time to Monday morning. The normal tariff was from 7s 6d to 12s 6d a day.

Cleveleys Hydro card party, *c.* 1930.

Apart from its famous remedial baths, Cleveleys Hydro boasted tennis courts and putting green and its fourteen-hole golf course which, just before the First World War was enlarged to become an eighteen-hole course.

In an advertisement in *Blackpool Gazette News* on 27 December 1907, publicizing the opening of the new Italian wing, Cleveleys Hydro is described as an 'ideal centre, especially for convalescents', and in the summertime 'excursions in the surrounding countryside are most agreeable and Cleveleys Hydro is centrally situated'. 'Poulton, with its old stocks and whipping post, is well worth visiting,' we are told, 'and so is Fleetwood.' Thornton and Bispham are also attractive nearby villages within short walking distances. Cleveleys village, believe it or not, wasn't even mentioned. In the years that followed, Cleveleys Hydro became increasingly well known and many famous people stayed there, especially First Division football teams. One famous visitor in the late 1920s was Gene Tunney, the American undefeated world heavyweight champion.

When war broke out in September, 1939, Cleveleys Hydro was taken over by the Ministry of Pensions as their Pensions Issue Office before the Warbreck Hill headquarters were built, and it was in 1941, after the completion of Warbreck Hill, that the Hydro became a hospital for RAF officers. Afterwards it became a headquarters for the Ministry of Health and for the last two years or so before the bulldozers and demolition men moved in it was a hostel for civil servants.

I remember in 1956 or 1957 wandering around the deserted and doomed Cleveleys Hydro which I remembered in its great days. Structurally, it was a magnificent building and anyone who saw the thickness of the walls said something like, 'They don't build like that any more.'

The eighteen-hole golf course used to extend to Shore Road at Little Bispham and the first stretch to be taken over for housing was that part around Little Bispham. The section of the

Aerial view of Cleveleys Hydro.

Sign at the tram track side.

golf course on the south side of Anchorsholme Lane West was saved to become Anchorsholme Park. Most of the former golf course adjoining the Hydro buildings and the former tennis courts and putting greens now consists of houses and bungalows, but the actual site of the main Cleveleys Hydro building itself is waste land.

Soon after the demolition of the buildings in 1956 and 1957, there were plans for multi-storey flats on the Hydro site and since then there have been all kinds of plans discussed about how this valuable site should be used. If one looks now, it is obvious that there has been some kind of a large building there. It wasn't only a large building. It was a luxury hotel with potted palms in the lounge and a Max Jaffa-type of orchestra playing melodies from the First World War or, as I remember, playing tunes like 'Diane, 'Charmaine' and 'Valencia'. Indeed, the glory has departed, but those who remember Cleveleys Hydro in its great days will never forget it. No, never.

7 January 1972

Fylde Courting Customs

Thornton Cleveleys Gala has its origins well back in the last century, but the Fylde custom from which it stems, the annual selection of a May Queen, is one of obscure but very ancient origin and may have links with a pagan spring festival.

In medieval times this was, I imagine, about the only really democratic institution in the country, because the May Queen – the origin of the present gala Rose Queen – was chosen by a general vote of everyone in the village. The queen wore a richly decorated costume on May Day, the day on which the maypole was carried to the village green by a team of decorated oxen, followed by a crowd of invariably tipsy revellers, and morris dancers also were an important feature of the celebration.

Not all medieval customs, unfortunately, were as pleasant as May Day. Indeed, some were thoroughly barbaric, such as the old Shrove Tuesday custom of tying a cock to a stave driven in the ground and then throwing stones or sticks at it until the poor creature died. There was no RSPCA then.

There used to be a delightful St Valentine's Day custom of young couples choosing their 'true loves' for the ensuing year. A very jolly, let-your-hair-down affair, it started with the names of all the young people being written on separate slips of paper, which were then divided into two lots, male and female. The men then drew a name from the list of females and vice-versa. Oddly enough, the men, according to Porter's famous *History of the Fylde*, invariably claimed as their sweethearts for the year the girls whose names they had drawn. It seems crazy to us, but our ancestors obviously thought it was great fun and they wined and dined and danced for several days after the festivities of St Valentine's Day and the young men proudly displayed the tickets they had drawn from the love lottery.

To medieval yokels, this custom may have seemed somewhat complicated, so there was an alternative method of choosing a valentine, the simplicity of which precluded all criticism. The girl who wanted a valentine merely woke up on St Valentine's Day and looked out of her window or door. The first person she saw was regarded as the special selection of St Valentine himself provided, of course, that he was a man and that he was either a bachelor or a widower. Whether there was any appeal against St Valentine's choice we don't know.

Another old Lancashire custom and one not confined to the Fylde, were Wakes. We still have Wakes, of course, holidays that begin immediately after Whitsuntide and continue until early September, but the original Wakes were different. They originated in an ancient custom of the villagers gathering together on the evening before the birthday of a saint and spending the whole night in prayer and meditation. Needless to say, this was far too tough a discipline to last long and the custom soon became completely divorced from the church and it finished as a general spree, the principal features of which were dancing, feasting, drinking, singing and all-round promiscuity.

Another peculiar custom was the making of a dumb-cake. This took place on Midsummer's Eve and two unmarried girls who wanted husbands baked the cake together in complete silence. A third girl, also looking for a husband, then broke the cake into three parts and the three girls then slept with a piece of the cake under their pillows. During the night, if all the rules had been scrupulously followed, the girls were rewarded with the sight of their future husbands, but they were not allowed to speak to them. Similarly, a single girl who fasted on Midsummer's Eve and at midnight laid a clean cloth, with bread and cheese on it, and sat down at the table as though she intended to eat, would also be rewarded with a miraculous vision of her future husband. He was supposed to come in through the door on the stroke of midnight, bow to her and pretend to drink her health. He then disappeared. If the girl liked his appearance everything was fine; if she didn't there was nothing she could do about it except have a good cry. The fates had spoken.

If one wanted to know one's life expectancy, there was a much simpler way than by visiting a doctor. One cut a few hairs from one's head, threw them in the fire and one's expectation of life depended on whether they blazed up or smouldered.

These old customs seem harmless enough, but in the belfry at Bispham parish church there used to be a wooden frame which in earlier times had been a penance stool. The last to perform penance in this church and sit on the stool was a woman who lived until about 1830. A public penance was exacted by the church from all girls who had 'lost their reputations' and who desired pardon for their misdemeanours. The ceremony consisted of the girl parading the aisle of the church with a lighted candle in each hand, bare-footed and clothed in white. Jane Breckal of Poulton-le-Fylde was the last to undergo this ceremony in these parts and this was sometime between 1770 and 1810. Apparently the girl was so distressed that the custom was discontinued locally and it was never revived. Reading of this custom, I was reminded of seeing in the South of France in August 1944, when I landed there with the 7th American Army, French girls with their hair cut off because they had fraternized with German soldiers during the occupation. In some respects, people don't change much over the centuries.

14 January 1972

Plundering Jamaica Inn-style

I may be hopelessly wrong about this, but I have an idea that among the spate of old films shown all too frequently on television, the screen adaptation of Daphne du Maurier's *Jamaica Inn* hasn't been included. If I remember correctly this was a British film made during the last war and it starred, I think, Charles Laughton and Emlyn Williams as the two principal villains. I can't remember who had the female lead. Was it Joan Fontaine? It was the story of a girl in the middle of the last century who went to stay with a relative at an inn on the Cornish Coast and she soon found out that the inn was little more than the operational headquarters of experienced smugglers.

For those in search of flotsam, the Fylde Coast still has plenty to offer. There is, for instance, an ample supply of timber available throughout the year and in my young days there used to be a profitable hobby of picking up coins – and they were not all coppers – around the beach and promenade. In the days before there was a promenade at Cleveleys as we know it today, there used to be a sloping cobblestone wall which acted as a sea defence and especially in the autumn there was a rich reward for anyone willing to devote an hour or two to finding coins that were hidden among the stones and that had, I suppose, been lost by visitors during the summer.

Driftwood and coins are not to be compared with what used to be washed up on this coast last century, chiefly from wrecked ships. Probably the locals then were not as law-abiding as they are these days, but 'finding's keeping' was their motto, and they were only too glad to 'liberate' anything that came ashore.

On January 7, 1838, the barque *Ann Paley*, sailing from Liverpool to Lisbon, was caught in a tremendous storm off this coast, and all her crew members were lost. The wreck foundered off Cleveleys and 'though every precaution was taken to stop plundering, much of her cargo was seized by the natives', it was stated by the Blackpool correspondent of *The Preston Pilot*, a small four-page newspaper that cost $4\frac{1}{2}$d.

During the winter in those days, there were wrecks almost weekly off this coast. Even in June 1833, after a sudden storm, eleven wrecks could be seen stranded off various points on the Fylde Coast. In 1799, when the population of Blackpool was 700, what was described as a 'God-send' occurred when a ship was wrecked off this coast with a cargo of peas. Apparently many local people were almost starving at the time, and they lived on these peas for months.

The queerest of these wrecks was probably a ship carrying cargo of bottled beer and what followed, according to contemporary reports, was very similar to Compton Mackenzie's story *Whisky Galore*. On 8 January 1839, the *Crusader*, a ship of 584 tons bound from Liverpool to Bombay with a cargo of mainly cotton goods and silks, was wrecked off North Shore. The captain and crew of twenty-six got safely ashore in two of the ship's boats and according to Allen Clarke's *The Story of Blackpool Lifeboat*, published in 1910, what followed was that 'a great deal of the *Crusader*'s valuable cargo was carried off. The captain, along with two constables from Preston searched the Marton district particularly, and there found silks and cotton goods hidden in pig-sties, down wells and buried in gardens.' Five men were charged with theft and as they all refused to pay fines of from £2 to £10, they were all sent to the House of Correction at Preston.

Fleetwood lighthouse was erected in 1840 and there seems to have been fewer wrecks off Rossall and Fleetwood afterwards, though this, I suppose, may have been largely due to the increasing use of steam engines for ships.

The most gruesome flotsam ever washed up on this coast were bodies from the *Ocean Monarch*, a ship en route to America from Liverpool with 400 immigrants in 1848. This ship caught fire and only 100 passengers were saved. Many of their companions' graves may still be seen in Bispham and Lytham churchyards.

A man named William Stout, a Lancaster man, kept a journal in the early eighteenth century and he describes a wreck off Norbreck in 1702. Stout was a sailor and he describes how his ship, the *Employment*, after being captured by a French man-of-war and ransomed for

£1,000, came up the Welsh coast and made for the Isle of Man. Being inexperienced the mate ran the ship for Peel Island off Barrow but he missed his course and went aground at Rossall. An attempt was made to launch a boat but rough seas, lashed to a fury by a gale, prevented this. The crew managed to land safely and the ship's cargo of sugar and cotton was taken ashore by the crew, the cotton to Bispham church and the sugar to Squire Fleetwood's barn at Rossall Hall. Considering that in 1775, a lifetime after the wreck off Rossall of the *Employment*, there were only twenty cottages and no shops in Blackpool, one can understand what a barren and lonely coast the Fylde must have been.

Anyone who believes, by the way, that summers in the 'good old days' were one long series of hot weeks, will soon have their illusions shattered by reading Allen Clarke's *The Story of the Blackpool Lifeboat*. There were tremendous storms every winter without exception and some were so severe that they smashed chimney pots in Preston. As far as those memorable storms of the eighteenth and nineteenth centuries are concerned, 'fings ain't wot they used to be'.

21 January 1972

A Vast Land Sale

Sixty-eight years ago this year [i.e. 1904] an event occurred which, at the time, probably seemed of no importance. The Fleetwood Estate Ltd bought from Messrs Horrocks of Preston, the famous textile firm, what had previously been called the Thornton Estate. The transfer of deeds started in 1903 and conveyancing was finally completed on 11 February 1904. From that date stems the real growth of this district as we know it today, particularly of that part of this district which used to be called Cleveleys.

Oddly enough, most of the so-called Thornton Estate consisted of Cleveleys. The area involved started at Broadwater, north of Rossall, and its southern boundary was Ramper Road, now Victoria Road. Its eastern boundary consisted of Fleetwood Road, Burn Hall – now called Bourne Hall – and Four Lane Ends. Apart from a few isolated areas, such as Thornton Vicarage and its grounds, the Thornton Estate included everything inside those boundaries. Like a Roman fort, this area was walled. Its boundaries were denoted by grass covered earth walls or ramps – hence the name Ramper Gate and Ramper Road – and very short stretches of these ramps were to be seen until a few years ago on the north side of Victoria Road near Rowlands Lane.

The Towers, Cleveleys.

Interesting Notes on the

CLEVELEYS

COTTAGE

EXHIBITION

Catalogue of Cleveleys Cottage exhibition.

Until this vast area was absorbed by the Fleetwood Estate Company, it belonged to the Horrocks family of Preston. They had acquired it from the estate of Sir Peter Hesketh Fleetwood, who lived at Rossall Hall and after whom Fleetwood is named. The Horrocks family used the Thornton Estate chiefly for hunting and shooting and near the centre of the Thornton Estate was a shooting lodge named The Towers which at the turn of this century became the home of Alderman T.G. Lumb. Alderman Lumb, who died in 1953, was Mayor of Blackpool in 1926, was elected a Freeman of Blackpool in 1947 and was chairman of the Bispham and Norbreck Urban District Council before that authority was taken over by Blackpool at the end of the First World War. Mr Lumb was also a trustee of the Cleveleys Park Methodist church, a building he designed in 1906; he was the father of the idea of a City of the Fylde; and, last but not least, he was managing director of the Fleetwood Estate Company, a firm which is still in existence and which has its offices in Fleetwood, opposite the old railway station in Dock Street.

It was the Horrocks family who built The Towers – the building itself was demolished only a few years ago and the land is now a council-owned open space – and the lodge's resident gamekeeper was Kess Hodgkinson, a famous local character. He was helped by John Barnes, who lived the last thirty or forty years of his life in Rossall Road, Cleveleys. I knew John Barnes well and he died less than twenty years ago.

Apart from The Towers, most of the Thornton Estate consisted of fields, farms, woods and ponds. Farms on the Thornton Estate which belonged to the Horrocks family included Town End Farm, Burn Hall, Rowland, Whiteside, Banks, Cocks, Wyresdale and College Farm. Wyresdale Farm is still there, but the farm itself has been replaced by a new house, and College Farm at Rossall Beach is still more or less as it was in the days of Thornton Estate except, of course, for the fact that it was an isolated outpost miles from anywhere whereas today it is, apart from its north side, almost surrounded by housing estates.

As I say, the Fleetwood Estate wanted to develop their newly acquired area and they lost no time in doing this. The man primarily behind this development idea was Mr T.G. Lumb. Less than two years after the conveyancing had been completed, the Fleetwood Estate organized what was called a 'Cottage Exhibition' on their land. This was only the second exhibition of its kind to be held in Britain – the first was in Letchworth Garden City – and the organizers of the Cleveleys Cottage Exhibition wanted to develop what was to become Thornton Cleveleys along the same lines as Letchworth Garden City. Mr Lumb, as he told me many years later, had himself visited Letchworth and he had been mightily impressed by what he saw there.

The site chosen for the Cleveleys Cottage Exhibition – that was the name used – was an area of fields and it comprised what were afterwards Stockdove Way, West Drive and Whiteside Way. Prizes were offered building contractors for the best houses built at specified prices – mostly – believe it or not, around the £150 to £200 mark – and the showpiece of the exhibition was the 'Dutch Cottage' in West Drive. The exhibition needed a pavilion and this afterwards became the West Drive Park Club or, rather, the old, single-storey part of that club. The name Park Club and also Cleveleys Park Methodist church are both references to the 1906 exhibition and the word 'park' stayed.

By the spring of 1906 all the exhibition houses had been built and Cleveleys Park Cottage Exhibition was widely advertised in newspapers and magazines, especially those circulating in the north of England. Officials of the Fleetwood Estate wanted a VIP to open this exhibition and they invited Sir George Armitage, chairman of the Lancashire and Yorkshire Railway Company, to perform the opening ceremony. The railway at Thornton was part of that railway company and both the Fleetwood Estate and the Lancashire and Yorkshire Railway Company were confident their exhibition would be a big success. The invitation was accepted by Sir George. The Chairman of Fleetwood Estate Company was Colonel D. Abercrombie, after whom Abercrombie Road in Fleetwood is named, and one of the firm's directors was a Mr William Dronsfield after whom Dronsfield Road in Fleetwood is named.

It was the exhibition that, more than anything else before or since, really put Cleveleys on the map. It started an era of expansion that, apart from ten war years, has continued ever since. The Fleetwood Estate Ltd was a firm that, in 1906, was already well established in the Fylde and it had been founded in 1876 when it bought from the executors of Sir Peter Hesketh Fleetwood virtually all of Fleetwood. At first, the firm was called the Fleetwood Estate Company Ltd and it retained this name until 1901 when it expanded and increased its holdings, after which the name was changed to the Fleetwood Estate Ltd.

Sir Peter Hesketh Fleetwood used to live at Rossall Hall and his home became the Church of England Northern School in the 1840s and was subsequently named Rossall School. Sir Peter had unlimited confidence in the future of the port at the mouth of the River Wyre which was named after him. He was instrumental in getting the railway line extended there from Preston in 1840 and he had plans for converting Burn Naze into an industrial area long, long before the United Alkali Works arrived there with their soda ash and salt works in 1896.

Alas, vision and foresight were not enough and making a new town was too much for Sir Peter, financially speaking. His fortune vanished and he left for the South of England. What happened to him from then on I don't know. He wasn't penniless but he was relatively poor. His dream of a new port ruined him. Sir Peter was, judged by any standard, a most remarkable man.

In his days, the first forty years of the nineteenth century, the biggest single problem on the Fylde Coast was erosion by the sea and I remember as a boy when I paddled far out from Cleveleys at unusually low tides and examined the rotting trunks of trees, the remains of what had obviously been at one time a large wood or even a forest. There must still be plenty of people who remember when Uncle Tom's Cabin was a wooden structure on the cliffs,

The entrance to the Cottage Exhibition.

Partially built Dutch cottage (on the right-hand side).

considerably to the west of its present location. That original Uncle Tom's Cabin fell over the cliffs into the sea due to coastal erosion and nothing is more certain than that there wouldn't be a Fylde Coast as we know it today if various sea defence schemes had not been implemented. How well I remember one night in October 1927 when a memorable storm smashed Cleveleys Promenade to smithereens and flooded inland as far as North Drive, but the worst affected areas were around Ash Street, Fleetwood, where people were marooned in their bedrooms because of the flooding.

Sir Peter Hesketh Fleetwood was well aware of the problem of coastal erosion and he had a system of cobble-stone sea defences built from Rossall to Fleetwood. He also had a cobbled road built all around his vast estate and on fine days he would travel around Fleetwood – his Fleetwood – along this perimeter road and promenade. When this was impossible because of the weather, he drove in his carriage and pair along Rossall Lane to Fleetwood Road past Broadwater and into Fleetwood and this, indeed, remained the main approach road to Fleetwood until, in 1933, Lord Beatty presented Alderman G.M. Robertson, the Mayor of Fleetwood, with the town's charter and, at the same time, Broadway was opened, the main road between Rossall Road and Poulton Road, Fleetwood.

The secretary of the Fleetwood Estate for many years was Mr F.S. Clarkson, of Whiteside Way, Cleveleys (also choirmaster at St Andrew's Parish church, Cleveleys, for many years until well after the last war), and he once showed me a contemporary map showing the Thornton Estate as it was at the time it was purchased by the Fleetwood Estate Ltd from the Horrocks family of Preston in 1904. That would have been around 1948 or 1949 and it showed an area that was completely unrecognizable apart from a few names of roads and farms and the fact that the Blackpool and Fleetwood tramroad highway, as it was called, had then been recently finished.

After the Cleveleys Park Cottage Exhibition of the summer of 1906 a minor building boom started. After the First World War, the government introduced a then revolutionary scheme which everyone seems to have forgotten now, of subsidies for private houses, and this caused an even greater speeding up in the tempo of building in Thornton Cleveleys.

During the 1920s and 1930s hundreds of local fields and ponds and hedges vanished and most of what had been the Horrocks Estate before 1904 disappeared for good. Now even The Towers has been demolished and it is difficult or impossible to find any evidence of the huge building outside the main entrance of which was a magnificent fig tree which blossomed regularly but, of course, never produced fruit. Where once pheasants, partridge and hares had roamed and had been stalked by parties of guests staying at The Towers there are now houses, mostly bungalows. I wonder what dear old Sir Peter would have had to say about the fate of his land? Something very pointed, I'll be bound.

4 February 1972

A Schoolteacher at Twelve

It's odd how one apparently forgets things until, by chance, they are recalled to us by a name. I recently had a chat with an old school friend of mine, Jack Ball, of Maida Vale, Anchorsholme, and he mentioned several names of boys and girls I knew well at the Beach Road Primary School in the 1920s when I was a pupil there. I had forgotten them until Jack mentioned their names and then how clearly they came back to memory.

Similarly, I had apparently forgotten Nook House at Thornton until I was reminded of the name recently by an old resident. Ah, yes, I remembered it well enough then, and what a delightful green retreat it was in the days of high summer! It was near Thornton parish church Sunday school in Meadows Avenue, and it was approached by a lane running alongside the Sunday school. In the days of Vicar Thomas Meadows – from 1870 to 1908 – part of the barn at Nook House Farm was used as a Sunday school and before that a converted stable was a schoolroom. The schoolroom was what was known in those days as a dame's school and it accommodated ten children. The teacher was Miss or Mrs Janet Rhodes and this school was the only one in Thornton Cleveleys apart, of course, from Baines' Endowed School which was founded in the early eighteenth century.

After the passing of the Compulsory Education Act of 1870 what used to be called Thornton Board School was built in Church Road and part of that building now comprises the infants' section of what these days is called the Church Road Primary School. The old Board School of the 1870s was built for no less than ninety scholars though whether it was fully used in the 1870s I don't know.

A famous old Thornton resident, Mr Dick Wright, who died about twenty years ago, once told, me to my astonishment – and he wasn't pulling my leg – that he attended the old Board School and, like everyone else, left when he was eleven years of age. Dick, however, returned when he was either twelve or thirteen years of age. Was this because he was thirsting for academic honours? Hardly. The reason he went back to school, believe it or not, was because he was a bright boy and he was asked to do some teaching, and he jolly well did – and there were no complaints from the teachers or the parents! Dick Wright was a teacher at twelve years of age. Beat that!

Mention of Nook house Farm, Dick Wright and the days of old Thornton remind me of being told recently of an old resident who was talking to some boys. None of them knew what he meant. Once every boy in this district knew that the snig was another word for the common eel, and most of us caught them in local ponds and streams though, to be honest, I've never liked the things. Some 'snigs' were caught on night-lines and I can remember the days when they were caught with an eel spear, a queer trident-like device with prongs at the end. I don't think I've seen an eel spear since I was a lad of about ten. I once saw a huge eel caught by an eel spear in the brook near Marsh Mill, Thornton, and it had been captured when men were clearing the reeds.

Eels are some of the most astonishing things in the animal world. They find their way from local ponds and streams to the depths of the Sargasso Sea between the North and South Atlantic where they spawn. I once saw a large eel on farmland off Anchorsholme Lane when I went there with the late Mr Ted Fenton who lived in Bank Avenue (afterwards called North Drive). I have forgotten the time of the year it was but I remember Ted Fenton, to whose farm I ran across fields to collects eggs for my mother, telling me something of the strange habits of eels, and I remember wondering whether he was 'having me on'. How, after all, could an insignificant little thing like an eel travel overland and swim to the middle of the Atlantic? It sounded crazy then and it sounds crazy now, but it's nevertheless true.

About ten years ago, before Anchorsholme Lane was built up, I remember a motorist telling me that he was travelling along at night when he saw something wriggling across the road. He stopped and saw it was an eel. There was some floodwater at the time and the eel was swimming

Burn Naze Council School, Thornton.

towards the fields belonging to Marsh Farm. Eels look alright behind the glass of an aquarium but as a boy I always hated getting them on my fishing line. They were slimy, agile and unkillable. How anyone can eat the things is something I've never understood, but there's a big market for them, especially, of course, jellied eels in and around London. No, the very thought of eating eels jellied, smoked, braised, fried, steamed, boiled or grilled upsets me. To our ancestors, of course, eel pie was a great delicacy. They're welcome to it!

11 February 1972

West Drive, Cleveleys Park.

Abdul the Algerian

Looking back on my young days I seem, like everyone else my age, to remember summers as seemingly endless when, of course, it never rained and winters when the landscape looked exactly like Christmas cards: snow, robins and a cosy fire indoors. What is true, I'm sure, is that neither summers nor winters are what they use to be. It used to be a fairly common occurrence for the River Thames to freeze over in winter. I can't remember anything like that happening to the River Wyre or any other British river.

The worst winter I recall was that of 1939/1940, which was far more severe than anything we have had in the intervening years. The tram service had to be suspended, headquarters of the Ministry of Pensions at Rossall School – evacuated from London on the outbreak of war in September 1939 – used sledges to get mail to and from the Post Office in Fleetwood.

My father took a photograph of me dwarfed by snowdrifts 14ft or 15ft high in Queens Drive, near Little Bispham, and many people had to dig themselves out of their houses. Drifts of 10ft were common but the full story of those weeks has never been told because, for some reason, it was believed that such information would be of use to the enemy. The sea froze over – something I have never known happen here before or since – but that memorable winter was followed by the best summer weather I remember. The summer when, in May, the British Expeditionary Force was evacuated from Dunkirk and the summer in which I was under various shapes and sizes of tents in South Wales to be a soldier for king and country.

Believe it or not, winters can be extremely severe in North Africa and in Southern Italy, and I speak with some experience. I have seen snow ploughs working on the main railway line from Algiers to Tunis and it was in a rather seedy suburb of Algiers, a place called Ain Taya, that I met Abdul under most un-African conditions. He was a swarthy Arab, unkempt, dressed in rags and with a red fez on his head. He was a sinister looking cut-throat if I ever saw one and, let the truth be spoken, he ponged. He ponged from a long way off and his pong wasn't in the least like any after-shave lotion I have ever sniffed.

I met him in a café in Ain Taya in the winter of 1943 and he was surrounded by an evil-looking pack of Arabs, all trying to look like Robert Newton after some film director said 'Come on, Mr Newton, let's see a bit more evil in your expressions.' The Arabs were drinking coffee or, rather, what passed for coffee in those distant days, and they were warming themselves in front of a charcoal fire. I noticed Abdul asking for another cup of the dark brew called coffee and then I noticed something else – the barman 'laced' it with 'triple sec', a type of brandy. Now I knew that Mohammed in the Koran had forbidden the use of alcohol and, out of the corner of a black, beady eye, Abdul saw me watching him. He knew that I knew that he knew and so on. Was I British or American, Abdul asked, presumably to avoid the embarrassing subject of Mohammed's attitude to liquor. I told him.

His English accent was thick – about as thick as the walls around Fort Knox in the United States – but he seemed proud of it. He not only claimed acquaintance with Shakespeare's tongue, but he claimed first-hand knowledge of Shakespeare's land. He knew England, he said, because he had been there. That, I thought, is what 'triple sec' does for someone who looks as if he hadn't had a square meal for a year or two. I'd heard that one before and I made as if to terminate our beautiful friendship, but Abdul was on his mettle. Where did I come from, he asked? This was damned silly, but I told him Blackpool.

Abdul wrinkled his brows and thought furiously. 'Tower' he said to my astonishment and then, in what he thought was English, he began slowly to describe two, or was it three, piers going out to sea from the Promenade. I thought he might have seen an illustrated article about Blackpool in some French magazine he had found in a dustbin and I further thought his conversation was a prelude to cadging so I walked towards the door and I told him that I didn't really come from Blackpool but from a place called Cleveleys. Abdul didn't know that, I said, but Abdul contradicted me. His dark, dirty and unwashed countenance was 'sicklied o'er with a pale cast of thought', as Shakespeare said; Adbul seemed to think that in some way the honour of the entire Arab race was involved now. There was what is called a pregnant silence and then it happened. 'Bisham' he said, and that was the way he pronounced it. I was intrigued and mystified, but if Abdul wanted to play games he would have to abide by the rules. 'No,' I said, 'not Bisham.' Then, like Archimedes who saw the mysteries of the universe unfold in a flash of inspiration, Abdul said 'West Avenue' and he metaphorically pole-axed me. He meant, of course, West Drive.

How did he do that? Abdul apparently had spent a year or two in England around 1930 selling carpets – these Algerian carpet sellers were a very colourful sight in the days between the two world wars – and his itinerary included a stop at Preston for a week or two while be travelled around part of the Fylde Coast. He remembered West Drive, or West Avenue as he called it, because somebody there had bought a good quality carpet and they had apparently paid the price Abdul asked for it without quibbling. This staggered Abdul so much that he remembered the occasion thirteen years afterwards in a seedy café in Ain Taya near Algiers.

Now I can't be sure of this, but I suspected from what Abdul told me that I knew the very man who had bought the carpet. He was, according to Abdul, a very nice man – anybody would have been very nice who paid Abdul's price without quibbling – and he wore a flower in his jacket. I think that man was Mr Wilfred Sadler who lived in West Drive for many years and who died either during or just after the last war. He was a wholesale ironmonger and he travelled daily on the 8.14 train from Thornton to Manchester. Yes, I think he meant Mr Wilfred Sadler.

It was a few days or a few weeks after this that I was admitted to hospital with some tropical illness – no, Abdul couldn't be blamed for that – and while I was getting ready to enter 96 General Hospital I encountered Ron Westerman. Ron lived in Thornton and had attended, like me, Baines' Grammar School at Poulton-le-Fylde, and he had been in the accounts department of Thornton Cleveleys Council Offices when Mr Tom Eaton was the council's treasurer. I told Ron of my strange encounter with Abdul, the scruffy Arab who remembered West Drive, and Ron, then a sergeant in the Royal Artillery, told me... but that's another story altogether.

18 February 1972

What Excitement When Electricity Arrived!

I noticed recently a group of men working on huge new standards in Victoria Road, Cleveleys, which seem to dwarf the old standards which, in their day, seemed incredibly tall. The new standards will improve street lighting but there doesn't seem to be agreement between those who believe in the blue type of street lighting we have and the orange type that is to be found elsewhere – at Carleton, for instance. One of them is called high-pressure sodium, but I forget which is which. The new standards in Cleveleys Avenue have led to a drastically improved system of street lighting – formerly it left a good deal to be desired for a main road – and watching these huge standards being erected my mind went back to the days of 1926 when Thornton Cleveleys got is electrical supply.

The council's new electrical engineer was Mr A.G. Cooper, a man with a large hooked nose, strongly reminiscent of portraits of the Duke of Wellington, and he and his staff certainly had a hectic and harrassing time during the early days of electricity here.

I remember the days of the changeover from gas to electricity well and the wonderful feeling of switching on an electric light or switching on an electrical vacuum cleaner. The house in which I lived – and I still do – was wired for electricity by a local electrician, Mr Harry R. Banks, who had a shop at the junction of Kings Road and Victoria Road opposite what was then the Savoy Cinema and Café and is now the Fine Fare and the Lancastria Co-op supermarkets. At the time Harry Banks was organist at St Andrew's church, Cleveleys, and a year or two later he sold his business and went to work as an electrician with the then new ICI works at Thornton, formerly the United Alkali Company.

There are still one or two old gas standards to be seen in odd corners of Thornton Cleveleys, though none of them, I think, function these days. A couple are in Anchorsholme Lane East and one is to be seen down the 'ginnel' from Rossall Road to the Constitutional Hall. Those, and a few others, are the only remaining legacies of the days when the council's lamplighter went round the district on a bicycle, lighting, repairing, maintaining and extinguishing the gas lamps.

The really big changeover from gas to electrical street lighting took place after the last war when the council had a Street Lighting Committee with Cllr W.A. Chadderton as chairman. I don't suppose there is anyone living now who can remember when everybody used oil lamps.

It was in 1900, when Thornton Cleveleys became an urban district council and the then new Council Offices were the Rossendale Bungalow, now the Ashley Conservative Club, that Thornton Cleveleys had its first street lighting. Before that no streets were lit at all. Mr 'Bob' Swarbrick, a famous local character and a carter who lived for many years at Pointer House, Four Lane Ends, Thornton – now the site of the National Westminster Bank – went to St Annes to bring the first consignment of street lamps. That was around 1900 or a little later. Thornton parish church was still lit by oil lamps when the church's new vicar, the Revd C.N. Sergeant, arrived in 1908, and one of the first improvements he put in hand was to have gas lighting installed in the church. A few, a very few, local residents, had been getting gas supplies from Poulton-le-Fylde before 1906 when the gas works off Heys Street, Thornton – still there and not very much changed – were established.

In 1926 when electricity arrived here the chairman of the council was the Revd E.G. King, a man I remember well and a man who, in one respect at least, was years ahead of his time. He had enormous sideburns and a heavy moustache and protruding from all this mass of hair was a nose on which rested a pair of spectacles. One would have imagined that he would have had the honour of pulling the switch and turning the juice on, but that honour fell to Cllr Jacob Marshall. He pulled the switch and the council offices were lit up with hundreds – or was it thousands? – of coloured lights and a spotlight fell on the Four Lane Ends War Memorial which had been dedicated three years previously, in 1923. That switch didn't only light up the council offices and the war memorial. There were altogether 500 consumers in Thornton Cleveleys and, inevitably I suppose, there were plenty of power failures during those early days.

Electricity switching-on ceremony in Victoria Square, 1926.

How well I remember these occasions. Suddenly the lights would be extinguished and my father, with a torch, would ensure that lights in other rooms were in order. He would then climb up steps to examine the fuse-box and I well remember occasions when, no torch being handy, I held a candle while he peered at the fuse-box. No, that was all right. Was the main switch on? It was. There could then be only one explanation: there had been a power failure. This is the Sherlock Holmes formula of elimination and it always worked. There had been a power failure.

In those times of teething troubles for the new electricity undertaking at Thornton Cleveleys one church at least had its Sunday evening service blacked out without warning and an organist accompanied the singing with the aid of two storm-lamps which were held by his side by two members of the congregation. As baby-faced Mary Hopkin sang a couple of years ago, 'Those were the days my friend.' They certainly were.

25 February 1972

A Gruesome Relic of a Century-old Tragedy

As a small boy, I spent a lot of time in Thornton parish church graveyard, not, I hasten to add, because I was, as Keats wrote, 'half in love with easeful death', but because I went there to work. I went with trowel and helped my parents to maintain the grave of an aunt of mine who died in 1912 and who is buried there. There was always a carpet of magic crocus and snowdrops in the spring and I don't think there was a lovelier vista anywhere in the Fylde than the majestic drive, lined with elms, that led from Meadows Avenue to the old vicarage. The old vicarage where, as a small boy I spent many hours because my parents were both friendly with the Revd C.N. Sergeant, is still there but it is now used as an old people's home and most of the avenue of elms has disappeared because of various modernization schemes to the church.

Near the church in Meadows Avenue is Oulder Nook, still a delightful rural cottage, but in my younger days it had a thatched roof – the only house with a thatched roof in Thornton Cleveleys if I remember – and for some reason it was referred to by locals then as 'Granny Parr's Cottage.' In spring the garden of Oulder Nook was richly carpeted with spring flowers, with that old-world thatched cottage in the background. Soon after the last war, a fire destroyed that thatched roof and it was never replaced.

During my visits to Thornton graveyard I often played truant and rambled off on my own among the old graves, trying to decipher what it said on the stones. Names like Silcock, Waring, Hornby, Bond, Porter and Parkinson speak of families long associated with Thornton.

Last summer I told two little girls, both of whom attend the Northfold Primary School, Cleveleys, who were going to visit their grandmother in the old vicarage near Thornton parish

The vicarage, Thornton.

104

The parish church, Thornton.

church and both of whom enjoyed looking around the graveyard, that there was one unusual tombstone which had set in it a large glass marble – what people used to call a glass ally – and this marble had been swallowed by a Thornton girl over 100 years ago and it had killed her. It seems incredibly gruesome to us these days, but the marble was extracted and mounted in the headstone on the little girl's grave. I casually asked the two young girls whether they had found this grave? No, but their enthusiasm was very evident. Where is it? I couldn't remember exactly, but it was near the Meadows Avenue side of the graveyard, I said. They found it alright, and it fascinated them. It happened 102 years ago, in 1870, and Minnie Rushton was only two years of age when she choked by swallowing the glass ally. How she ever got it into her mouth is something I have never understood.

When I was a small boy I supposed every child around here knew this grave well. It was pointed out to us, probably, I suspect, as a warning. I was certainly warned by my parents about the danger of swallowing things – I was reminded of Minnie's terrible fate. Minnie's grave is difficult to find – it always was – because it is well away from the path, is among old graves and it is, or rather was when I last saw it many years ago, screened by evergreen bushes. I don't suppose many people bother to look for it now, I don't suppose many people have heard of it. Once it was bordered by ferns but I can visualize it now as I remember it long, long ago dark and mysterious and with fallen holly leaves on the grave. And surely ... yes, surely I am right that there used to be a rambling rose tree sprawling over the headstone.

Who Minnie Rushton was I don't know, where her parents lived I don't know, and nobody bothered tending her grave as my aunt's grave was tended. Poor little Minnie's grave was hidden away in a very 'spooky' part of the graveyard and nobody bothered with her, except kids like me who stared in awe and a kind of cold fear at that glass ally set in the headstone. Never do I remember seeing a bunch of flowers on poor Minnie's grave, but by the time I visited her grave Minnie had been dead for over fifty years. I wonder how many people who visit relatives' graves in Thornton churchyard have ever heard of Minnie Rushton or seen the rather gruesome glass ally in her headstone?

Another tombstone not very far away from Minnie's – it also takes some finding – bears an inscription that commemorates another sad story. It is dated 1869 and records the death by drowning of two Rossall schoolboys. They came from Ireland and their names were James Morton Ruxton Fitzherbert Olden, the only son of the Vicar of Ballyclough, County Cork, and his cousin, Robert Morton Aidworth, a son of Major Aidworth, of Cork. The two boys went out to bathe outside regulation hours somewhere near Rossall School and they were cut off by the ever-deepening channel which engulfed them as they tried to struggle back. That is another forgotten grave in another obscure corner of Thornton parish church graveyard, but at least one thing has remained unchanged since the days of Minnie Rushton and those two Irish boys from Rossall School: the sea is just as treacherous as it was then and it will remain treacherous. Alas, how many lives, especially young lives, could and would have been saved if they had learned this lesson.

3 March 1972

Dick Crookall Wanted to be an Engineer

Vast changes are now taking place in one of the few country lanes that, until last year, had barely altered over the years. Opposite the main entrance to Rossall School, Rossall Lane is being developed as a huge housing area and it obviously won't be long before that lane is quite unrecognizable. Already it is busy with traffic travelling between Fleetwood and Cleveleys, but I remember it when it was one of the loneliest lanes anywhere around here and, apart from the odd horse-drawn farm cart, the only people who used it regularly were Rossall schoolboys who, especially in spring and autumn, used to run along this lane and through Thornton village playing hares and hounds.

Some of my earliest memories are of those Rossall boys in the days when Canon Houghton was headmaster, but Rossall boys in those days belonged to a closed community. They didn't mix with people outside the school nor were they encouraged to do so. They lived an almost monastic life and only left the school for their strange form of hockey on the sands – a game peculiar to Rossall – and for their hares and hounds. Those running Rossallians form in some strange way an integral part of my childhood and I suppose I had an unusual link with the school because when I was about five my parents were friendly with a Mr Wilson, a master at the school, and they occasionally visited his house inside the school boundaries.

Until the last war, Rossall School was regarded as the last outpost before the long and deserted stretch tapering off to the peninsular where, in the days of my boyhood, there used to be a huge wooden landmark, something to do with guiding ships, between Rossall School and Fleetwood. That was demolished in the 1920s. The construction of a modern seawall in the 1930s made the formerly lonely stretch between Rossall and Fleetwood more accessible, but few people ever bothered walking along there. What a change these days! The spread of Fleetwood's housing estates has completely obliterated all traces of the incredibly lonely stretch between Rossall School and Fleetwood.

From Cock's Farm, where a film actress named Belle Chrystall lived as a schoolgirl, the open flat fields stretched all the way to West Drive, Cleveleys. Nowadays Pheasant and Woodcock Woods remain as the only two relics of the days when this vast expanse of land was stocked with game and The Towers, off Holmefield Avenue, was a shooting lodge. Larkholme Farm has completely disappeared now – that was about the loneliest farm I have ever seen – and Fleetwood's pumping station, which use to stand in splendid isolation, is now completely surrounded by houses and bungalows.

People today will find it impossible to believe how isolated that pumping station was in the 1920s before the Sunshine Home, now Rossall Hospital, was built in around 1930. Farmer Dick Crookall, for so many years a member of the Sacred Heart church at Thornton where Father J. Bamber was the priest, was born at Larkholme Farm but, because of inundations by the sea, his parents had to leave the farm and that was how the family came to build Springfield Farm just north of the boundary between Thornton Cleveleys and Fleetwood over Bourne Hill.

The site of Springfield Farm is now a huge caravan site near the junction of Fleetwood Road North and Rossall Lane. It must be about twenty years since I was travelling along this stretch of Fleetwood Road North when I saw the uprooting of orchard trees that had been part of Springfield Farm to make way for the caravan site. I felt sad at the passing of the old and familiar and there are certainly no orchard trees around there now.

This part of our district was rural and lonely in the days of the old United Alkali Company's salt works at the rear of Springfield Terrace which, for some reason or other, used to be called 'Burglars' Alley'. Bourne Hall Farm, Springfield Terrace, the Saltworks and Springfield Farm, that's how the progression northwards went from Thornton. Now, of course, it's the huge Organics Division of the ICI and the big caravan camp instead.

To return to Dick Crookall, a man whom everyone in Thornton knew well. He died after the last war and for many years he was a Fleetwood councillor and he became chairman of Fleetwood Urban District Council before borough status was attained in 1933. When Earl

Beacon at Rossall Point, 1921.

Beatty presented Alderman G.M. Robertson with the town's charter, I was there, standing on my toes to get a glimpse of the almost legendary Earl Beatty the sight of whom I may add, didn't disappoint me. He looked exactly what he was, a seaman in the Nelson mould.

I remember Dick Crookall once telling me that in the great days of this area as a wheat growing district, he accompanied cartloads of grain to Preston for sale in the market. He also brought huge quantities of wheat to be ground at Thornton's Marsh Mill and I suspect he must have been the last man who really thoroughly knew the mill in its original role. Dick Crookall, strangely, didn't want to be a farmer when he was a boy, though he always impressed me as a born farmer. He wanted to be an engineer but his father had other ideas so he had to turn down the offer of a job with the Lancashire and Yorkshire Railway Company. Maybe he fancied the railway as a career because he was only a child of five or six years of age when his father built Springfield Farm and lads in those days, I'll be bound, got a real thrill out of steam engines. He told me that himself about twenty-five years ago and I believed him. I used to feel the same way about steam engines. I loved them, and I defy anyone to feel that way about a soulless hunk of steel called a diesel engine.

7 April 1972

Students were a Tough Lot

Are young people today bad mannered, ill-educated, lacking in respect for their elders, arrogant and contemptuous of all authority? It's a good subject for debate, of course, but opposing speakers, I suspect, will never agree however long they discuss this subject. The popular idea seems to be that young people these days are a mob of illiterate and ill-disciplined oafs and I feel sure that if Dr Gallup's volunteers stopped a couple of hundred people at random here or elsewhere, most adults would say that young people today are not as good as they were say 50 or 100 years ago. I've heard that line or argument often enough – so has everybody else – but I'm far from convinced that it is true. 'It's more discipline the so-and-so's want' is a statement heard every day in homes, cafés, pubs, shops and offices.

And yet, when Byron, whom the Continent has always regarded as the greatest of our Romantic poets, was at Harrow School he was implicated in a plot to blow up the entire school with barrels of gunpowder and Shelley, Byron's contemporary, not to put too fine a point on it, made life hell on earth for his tutors at Oxford. In Yorkshire in 1911, a schoolboy was charged with the attempted murder of one of his schoolmasters.

I often hear the behaviour of Rossall schoolboys praised and a sound case could be made out that the present students are a great deal better behaved than they were a century ago. Rossall School was opened as the Church of England Northern School in 1844 and its first headmaster was the Revd Dr John Woolley, who stayed from 1844 to 1849. Although a scholar and a gentleman, he was apparently a lax disciplinarian and he was not interested in the establishment of a tuck shop at the school – that came with Dr Woolley's successor, the Revd William Alexander Osborne, who stayed at Rossall from 1849 to 1870. In Dr Woolley's time, pastry cooks from Fleetwood relieved the boys of most of their surplus spending money, and not only did they sell pastries. They also sold spirits, beer, tobacco, matches and – believe it or not – gunpowder was smuggled into the school.

During Dr Osborne's reign as headmaster there was a rebellion by the monitors who, believing they were being burdened with unnecessary duties, went to see Dr Osborne and they resigned as a body. The conspirators' headquarters was the school library, and while they were preparing, Dr Osborne walked in ostensibly in search of a book he had forgotten. When the monitors delivered their ultimatum to Dr Osborne he told them: 'Gentlemen, you are monitors and you will continue to be monitors.'

These and other delightful stories about the early days of Rossall School are told in *Rossall School: Its Rise and Progress* by Canon St Vincent Beechey, a privately printed book published in 1894 which I bought during the last war at a second-hand bookshop in Portsmouth near the Guildhall, then recently demolished by German bombs. Canon Beechey was Vicar of Thornton from 1841 to 1856 and he was the founder of Rossall School. He was also the first Vicar of Fleetwood. From 1842 to 1872 he was secretary of Rossall School. Canon Beechey's life spanned most of the nineteenth century and his book, though fairly short, contains a wealth of fascinating local history concerning Rossall, Thornton and Fleetwood. He was a close friend of Sir Peter Hesketh Fleetwood, the founder of Fleetwood, who lived at Rossall Hall.

Rossall is first heard of in the thirteenth century when the hall there was swept away by the sea. A later, rebuilt, Rossall Hall was the home of the Allen family, the most famous member of which was the Elizabethan Cardinal Allen who founded the English College at Rome and which is still famous as a training college for Roman catholic priests. Thornton is mentioned in the *Domesday Book* and so is Carleton, Cleveleys, alas, isn't heard of until the eighteenth century.

Anchorsholme Hall, demolished a few years ago, was a former shooting lodge like The Towers off Holmefield Avenue, and Princess Louise, daughter of Queen Victoria, spent her honeymoon at there. Norbertine monks from Cockersands Abbey used to farm land in and around Thornton, including the land on which now stands the headquarters of the Department of Health and Social Security at Norcross. Yes, there's a wealth of history in and around

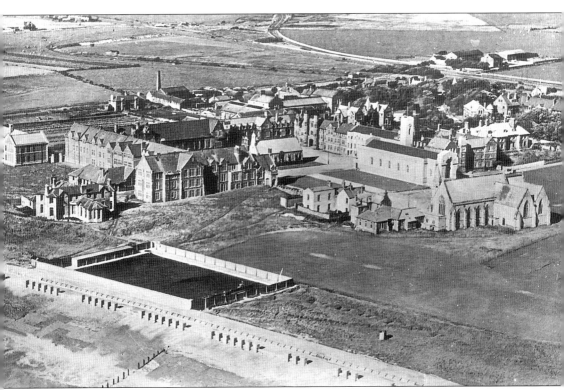

Rossall School, Fleetwood.

Thornton Cleveleys and plenty of people, I'm sure will be delighted at the recent news that there is to be a local history exhibition staged to coincide with Thornton Cleveleys Gala fortnight in June. Where's this history exhibition to be held? In the best of all possible local sites for such an exhibition in Marsh Mill, Thornton, built in 1749. Though it ceased to be a working corn mill just over fifty years ago, it is still going strong and is still the most famous of all local landmarks.

14 April 1972

The parade at Cleveleys.

Clerks and Cricket

In the early 1920s the government introduced a scheme for house subsidies – nobody these days seems to have heard of it – and this led to a major building boom in Thornton Cleveleys by such local building firms as Cryer, Gillett, Holt and Dawson and Fletcher. Most houses, other than corner properties, were on sale for £395 and I think I am correct in saying that the actual cash needed to buy a new house then was £20. The rest could be borrowed from a building society, given security. A vast number of houses were built in Thornton Cleveleys for £395 – it seemed to be a more or less standard charge for a semi-detached house – and I have been in hundreds of those houses when they were being built.

I don't know whether boys today love to clamber around in houses being built as I did, and the fact that this can be dangerous only adds to the excitement. Some of the happiest hours of my boyhood were spent exploring houses in the course of erection after the builders had left or on Sundays.

This housing boom meant, among other things, an increase in the staff at Thornton Cleveleys Council Offices and around 1924 or 1925 it was decided the staff was large enough to field a cricket team. The late Mr Fred Goddard of Henley Avenue, Cleveleys, a member of the surveyor's department for many years, could tell some marvellous stories about this team, most of whom were volunteers but a few of whom, in emergencies, had to be coerced into putting on the pads and trying to emulate Sutcliffe, Hobbs, Kilner, Hirst and other famous English cricketers of their day.

First impressions are important and the cricketers had to look the part so the team borrowed gaudy caps used by morris dancers at annual gala days which were stored at the council offices. Whether Miss Mary Lingard, the trainer of the Thornton morris dancers, knew about this, I don't know; I very much doubt it. They must have looked a rum bunch and, according to Fred Goddard, they were a rum bunch. Joe Walker, the building inspector, was the team captain. How long these cricketers used their colourful headgear I don't know, but annually the council offices team found they could draw on an increasingly bigger pool of manpower, and it wasn't many years before members of our volunteer fire brigade issued a challenge, not to fight a fire but to fight a cricket match.

The fire brigade's team, I believe, was then a new or a relatively new one and I believe some men were, as it were, made honorary local firemen for the duration of a cricket match. The late Fred Goddard, a man personally involved, told me of the duel which took place in a field off Fleetwood Road where the then Primitive Methodist church's team played. Whether on this particular occasion the firemen had 'signed on' any temporary firemen for the afternoon I know not, but the firemen failed. The 'office blokes' were victorious. Let the whole truth be told, however. Fred Goddard told me that the council offices' victory was primarily due to two new men, himself and Harold Benson, who, if I remember correctly, got at least three-quarters of the runs. There were plenty of ducks that day and not feathered ones.

The council offices team included Ken Parker, Dick Unsworth, Tom Eaton, Joe Walker, Frank Croker, Billy Clarke and Harry Carpenter and, I think, Clifford Longton. How some of those names bring back memories. Ken Parker went to Rhodesia either before or just after the last war and he used to live at Brianholme, South Promenade, Cleveleys. He had a sister, Mary, and another sister, Cheryl, who became locally famous as secretary of Thornton Cleveleys Old People's Welfare Association.

I used to go to Baines' Grammar School with Dick Unsworth, whose brother, another contemporary of mine, had a chemist's shop in Lawsons Road, Thornton. I knew Clifford Longton well and I used to attend West Drive Methodist church Sunday school with him and his brothers Alfred and Harry. Just after the First World War their parents opened a sweet and tobacconists shop on what was to become The Parade, Cleveleys, and around 1930 they opened a confectioners near what is now the RAF Association headquarters. I last heard of the family about twenty years ago when they all left for New Zealand. Billy Clarke lived over Wyre, Harold Benson became the council's treasurer and accountant, and succeeded Mr Tom Eaton, and Harry Carpenter was Blackpool Illuminations chief. Joe Walker, Fred Goddard and Tom Eaton, alas, are all dead.

What about the vanquished, the challengers? Some of their team consisted of Eli Burgess, Harry Jones, Bill Fletcher, Ernie James, Harry Swarbrick, Dick Roskell, Wilf Jackson and others whose names Fred Goddard couldn't recall. Soon after this memorable clash, the teams met again for a second and final encounter. This time the firemen won a comfortable victory, so honours were even.

21 April 1972

Plenty of Talent

Worth pondering over sometimes are the good things that emerged from the last war – there were some – and high on the list was a quite fantastic revival of interest in the amateur dramatic and allied movements. The tremendous impetus that the war gave to these movements outlasted the war years, but is that interest as evident now as it was in the 1850s? Why should the war have stimulated interest in amateur theatricals? People had far less spare time then than they have now and it's difficult to reconcile two such apparent opposites as a war and amateur theatricals but there was a close relationship between them.

For reasons that aren't easy to understand, amateur dramatic societies spring up everywhere almost overnight and apart from the keenness and enthusiasm of the members themselves, there was a genuine public interest in their activities and a willingness to support them financially. In Thornton Cleveleys the Amateur Operatic Society started in 1938 as the Amateur Operatic and Dramatic Society, the Windmill Players started in 1945, the Aitkin Players started at about the same time, the Norcross Players started here in 1940 as the Ministry of Pensions Amateur Dramatic Society and I think the Wignall Dramatic Society started during the last war. They certainly became well known locally during and just after the war. Some of the societies have folded, including the Arts Repertory Company, originally part of the Operatic Society.

These amateur societies have a record to be proud of. They have done a lot for this district: they have raised money for charities, they have given pleasure and entertainment to thousands of people and they have brought out plenty of acting talent which would otherwise have remained undiscovered. That's quite an achievement. Though, as I have said, some societies have folded – who remembers the pre-war choral society and the Norcross Crown Revels? – other societies like the Junior Theatre (now renamed the Youth Theatre) have arrived on the local scene to replace them.

For a place the size of Thornton Cleveleys, the story of these amateur societies has been a remarkable one, but all of them still in existence are faced with increasing costs and the difficulty of finding suitable halls to stage and rehearse their shows. If anyone doubts the extent of the immediate post-war enthusiasm for amateur societies here, let them remember that just after the war ended a small society, the Theatre Guild, was formed and in a little over two years they amassed a bank balance of £500. That, in today's terms, represents I suppose about £2,000.

Local amateurs then believed – and I am thinking particularly of people like Fred Goddard, Hartley Watts, H.G. Rae, C.R.O. Taylor, J.F. Tattersall and Ethel Aitkin – that Thornton Cleveleys would soon have a theatre of its own where local amateur productions could be staged. That, I suppose was the chief reason why £500 was raised in two years by the local Theatre Guild. That dream has faded and now it's a mirage. Basically, the amateurs' chief problem is finance and every show a group of amateurs stage costs more that their previous show and there are limits to what the public will pay in the way of increased ticket charges. Increased costs also mean that amateurs must play safe with their selection of players and shows, but is contrary to the whole spirit of the amateur stage which should be characterized by boldness, a willingness to experiment and a refusal to let their treasurer have the final word about anything. It's bad for amateurs to be compelled to play safe. It inhibits enthusiasm and acts as a cold douche on members who would like to have a crack at lesser-known shows, but will the public support these?

Amateurs have more than their fair share of problems these days, but I have seen some splendid local shows over the years presented by our local companies and one of the last local shows I attended was Gilbert and Sullivan's *Princess Ida* by the Youth Theatre. Like many people, I have seen G and S shows like *The Mikado*, *The Pirates of Penzance* and *The Gondoliers* often enough, but I have never seen *Princess Ida* before. In my opinion it is a brilliant combination of music and story and the Youth Theatre, also in my opinion, have never done anything better since they grew out of the Cleveleys Songsters' Society founded by Miss Olive Clipsham. One thing that delighted me about my visit to *Princess Ida* was to see a full Lecture Hall.

The public, alas, seems to be losing interest in the amateur stage and television appears to be replacing it, but my experience is that no television screen, even if it's 50 square inches, and aluminized twenty times and has stereophonic sound and colour, can compare with what's called the legitimate stage. The stage has a strange magic of its own which goes back to the days of Ancient Greece. This magic isn't easy to define but it is easy to recognize. The cinema screen and the television screen can offer a lot but they miss a lot too. They're not 'live' as the stage is.

I admire our local amateurs unreservedly. They work hard and unselfishly and they've put on some grand shows here – as they still do. Alright, it's agreed that some of the actors occasionally make mistakes, but it's also true that some of them, remember, can act a great deal better than many of the famous names on the British stage and screen. Think of some of the dismal, so-called acting that one sees in television plays where the actors and actresses are professionals. I have seen plenty of weak productions by local amateurs; I wouldn't attempt to deny that, but I have also seen local amateurs who were capable of acting the pants off some of the so-called 'stars' of the television screen. What about my old friend Lance Gray of the Arts Repertory Company? He could act in comedy, farce or high drama and he was always thoroughly convincing whatever his role.

28 April 1972

Calling a Woman a Witch was No Joke

Well do I remember Mr R. Sharpe-France, the Lancashire County Council archivist, speaking to members of Thornton Cleveleys Rotary Club at one of their weekly meetings and telling them that it was quite certain that people have been walking the lanes of Thornton for well over a thousand years. That, I think, is worth bearing in mind by those schoolchildren and adults who will be visiting the local exhibition at Thornton to coincide with this year's fortnight of gala celebrations in June. I remember Mr Sharpe-France passing around a selection of rare documents, mostly relating to old Thornton, and they included an allegation of witchcraft against a woman from Skippool. That was in 1627. Nobody knows, of course, when Thornton's history started but it certainly started before the *Domesday Book*, in which Thornton is first mentioned, was compiled in 1086. That's long, long before there was any Blackpool or Fleetwood.

The witchcraft document Mr Sharpe-France showed Rotarians was dated 12 December 1627, and was a complaint to the magistrates, submitted by Dorothy Shaw, wife of Thomas Shaw, a joiner of Skippool, alleging that William Wilkinson of Skippool had called her a witch. Mr Wilkinson was called and told to behave himself in future and not to repeat those baseless slanders.

I suppose it would be a minor joke now to call a woman a witch, but it was no joke in the seventeenth century. It was about the most serious allegation one could make against a woman. This, after all, was only eighteen years after the famous Lancashire witches' trial which was the subject of a famous historical novel by Harrison Ainsworth, the nineteenth-century historical novelist.

In 1698 the inhabitants of Thornton were warned that unless they improved their sluices, maintained the King's Highway in a proper state and prevented flooding from the sea they would, in future, incur a collective fine of £60. They were also given a deadline, a date by which the work had to be completed. In 1704 Henry Hall, a local miller, with a wife and five children, asked permission to build a cottage on Thornton Marsh. Henry Hall stated that he had lived in Thornton for twenty-eight years and he had drawn about £1 annually from the rates because he and his family had no proper living accommodation.

He promised that if the cottage was forthcoming he would no longer be a burden on the parish and, because of this undertaking, permission was granted and a site was allocated him by Richard Fleetwood of Rossall Hall. Henry Hall, however, afterwards complained that after he had received permission to have his cottage John Westby of Bourne Hall, Thornton, had stopped work proceedings with the building of the cottage. During this time, Henry Hall was living in a neighbour's barn, and the magistrates awarded him a shilling a week until his cottage was ready. Presumably they overruled any action taken or threats made by Mr Fleetwood of Rossall, a predecessor of Sir Peter Hesketh Fleetwood, the founder of Fleetwood in 1840.

An inventory taken of the goods owned by Lawrence Hull of Thornton in 1675, then recently died, showed a feather bed and bolster valued at 30s, the bedclothes and sheets valued at 25s, linen napkins at 10s, his wife's clothes at 29s, half a cow – he shared the cow with either his brother or a neighbour – £1 15s, three steers £8 10s 6d, and loose money £9 7s 6d. His own clothes were valued at £1 4s 6d. I find old documents like these of endless fascination and it's a safe bet that plenty of them will be on display at Thornton's Marsh Mill in June.

5 May 1972

Bourne Hall.

Boyhood Days in 1920s Thornton

A lieutenant-colonel in the US Air Force now serving in West Germany, Charles H. Freudenthal, is the younger son of the late Mrs Rachel Greenhalgh Holt who grew up in Thornton. Mr Freudenthal and his brother lived for several years during the 1920s in Thornton, firstly in Crabtree Road and then in Meadows Avenue, and he has written some of the recollections of those bygone years. 'I remember, I think above all, the sweet delicate smell of the blackberry bushes in the meadows around the parish church. They started, if I recall, near the entrance to Stockdove Wood and often my brother and I and Bernard Knowles would spend a warm afternoon there picking the ripe berries. Sometimes armed with a glass jar and a damp rag, we would catch bees and take them home to wait, hopefully, for honey. We never got any.

There are many other things I remember about Thornton, though it's over forty years since I last walked home to my grandmother's house in Meadows Avenue; not the names of the streets nor of people come back to me, but I can tell you what we did and where. Twilight, for instance. This meant teatime, the sharp slamming of gates and an end to games. Mothers – grandmother in my case – called us home and put an abrupt end to football games, bicycle rides, discussions and arguments.

I remember the *Boy's Own* magazine because my brother, two years older than me, was usually entrusted with my twopence allowance as well as his, and he would spend it first on magazines. Only when his reading needs had been met was I able to go to the little candy store

Thornton church.

Outside the vicarage the vicar with ladies of the church, 1955. From left to right, standing: Mrs C. Whittaker, Mrs H. Butcher, Mrs Godwin, Mrs G. Dickinson, Mrs Wood, Mrs Bolton, Miss R. Bowlass (now Mrs J. Woods) and Miss Preston (now Mrs J.R. Hull). Seated: Mrs Whittakar, the vicar C.N. Sergeant, Miss Sergeant, Mrs J. Preston and Miss R. Jagger.

near the old windmill. Liquorice allsorts were my favourites with penny 'lucky bags' close second. I remember getting these at a little shop on Marsh Road when my Uncle Wally gave me a penny for getting Woodbine cigarettes for him.

Now all this took place a long time ago and I have forgotten a lot, but I remember the stack of pennies we kept to put in the gas meter when the lights started to flicker, and lighting myself to bed with a candle, breakfasts of porridge, gooseberries fresh off the bushes, and russet apples, and I mustn't forget treacle toffee or parkin on Guy Fawkes night.

Perhaps my memories have been shaped and mellowed by time, but they are the better for it, I'm sure. Thornton can't possibly be the same today and no doubt I'd be better off not coming back to find out. If I did come back would I see the pierrots on the beach at Cleveleys and the man with the donkeys at a penny a ride? To be honest, my brother and I seldom paid a penny for a ride. Pennies were not too easy to come by in those days and if we timed it right we could get a free donkey ride when the owner led the donkeys down Victoria Road. I don't remember his name but I send my belated thanks for the rides to him.

I remember my job with a man who sold fruit around Thornton and Cleveleys. I wasn't ever really hired, I just decided I would like to ride around with this man who visited so many places. So one day as he went by I hopped on the step at the back of his cart and became his employee. He took it all in good spirits and while we didn't talk to each other much, it was soon understood that I was allowed to weigh potatoes and could deliver packages to customers. These were wonderful, long, sunny days and there was no pay asked for or given, except an occasional apple, but the pace was slow and there was time to daydream. We went, this tall, gaunt and bespectacled man with his straggly moustache and his seven-year-old assistant, along Meadows Avenue, Four Lane Ends, Victoria Road and God knows where else.

I remember picking apples and pears in the orchard of Thornton church rectory – by invitation, mind you. The minister was the Revd C. N. Sergeant and he used to invite local youngsters to help him pick his fruit and to eat all we wanted to for doing so. He was a kindly man. Besides going to this church every Sunday I voluntarily attended many funerals there and could tell anyone who cared to listen exactly how things were going and what would happen next. There was a stile near our house in Meadows Avenue where I perched to view the happenings.

I wonder if the big field is there along the road to the council offices where they held gala days. Do the Territorials still drill near the church? Could it have been my uncle's regiment, the Royal North Lancashires, that were there? At any rate, they certainly taught boys in the neighbourhood to 'form fours'.

I could go on for hours remembering the Thornton I knew. I remember collecting cigarette cards and birds' eggs, but I also remember that I was never able to get a complete set of the life of Napoleon in cigarette cards. I remember Frank Croft whose father had a butcher's shop in Cleveleys; Miss Lonsdale, who taught us French at Castlemaine School; Bernard Knowles and Mr Smythe, the headmaster of Cleveleys College. My grandmother's house in Meadows-avenue was named Church Bank. How big and new it was then.

I remember so much from those days but, especially I think, do I remember Thornton for the summer days there. I don't seem to have any strong recollections of winter there except for football games and, of course, for Christmas. Christmas was, and is, something special. There was an air about Christmas that just won't slip away. Perhaps it was all the good things to eat, but I don't think so, really. Maybe it was the oranges with sixpenny pieces in them or the biscuits and the stockings full of nuts and raisins and apples, or perhaps a shiny half-crown. More likely it was all these things coupled with a shaky yes-I-do, no-I-don't belief in Father Christmas. Maybe, after all, it's because it was in Thornton.'

5 October 1973

T.G. Lumb: Man of Vision

At least a dozen men played prominent parts in the development of Thornton Cleveleys before the First World War and in the 1920s, but one name in particular stands out: Mr T.G. Lumb, who died at the age of ninety-one in 1953.

After being articled with a firm of Manchester architects, he joined the old Lancashire and Yorkshire Railway company and then a Preston firm of civil engineers. In 1892 he was appointed Blackpool manager for that Preston firm. He spent the rest of his long life on the Fylde coast.

He prepared plans and supervised construction of the Blackpool and Fleetwood tramway system which opened in 1898, and he told me many times in his later years that he liked riding on the trams then and that it was during these trips that he had a vision that never left him: a City of the Fylde stretching from Lytham to Fleetwood. It must have seemed a crazy idea in the 1890s. The young T.G. Lumb believed there was an enormous future awaiting the Fylde coast if only it could be developed.

Most of the coastline then consisted of sandhills. There were only a handful of houses and farms at Cleveleys. Between Rossall School and Cleveleys there was College Farm and between Rossall School and Ash Street, Fleetwood, there were fields and a few allotments; nothing else.

In 1900, Mr Lumb started in business on his own and was invited to join a syndicate of businessmen, known as the Fleetwood Estate Company, to purchase 1,000 acres from the Horrocks Estates. The Thornton Estate, including the 1,000 acres mentioned, totalled well over 2,000 acres. That huge tract of land now belonged to the Fleetwood Estate Company and a start was made on developing part of it at Rossall Beach and Thornton Gate.

Helping young Mr Lumb to develop this was a young architect, Mr E.L. Lutyens, afterwards Sir Edwin Lutyens, designer of the Menin Gate and the Viceroy's Palace at Delhi. Mr Lutyens designed several houses at Rossall Beach including one, Beach Croft, in which Mr Lumb lived for some time. Soon afterwards Mr Lumb moved to The Towers at Cleveleys, previously a shooting lodge owned by the Horrocks family of Bolton who had bought the Thornton Estate from Sir Peter Hesketh Fleetwood, founder of Fleetwood, who lived at Rossall. The Towers had over 100 acres of land rich in grass and with a gamekeeper. Mr Lumb kept the shooting rights enjoyed by the Horrocks family and I remember him telling me of some of the shooting parties there before the First World War, when the estate was rich in pheasant, partridge, snipe, wild duck and hares.

Lumb was determined to put Cleveleys on the map and the result was the Cleveleys Cottage Exhibition of 1906, a spectacular success. Houses were built to specific prices in Cleveleys Park, which comprised West Drive, Stockdove Way, Whiteside Way and part of Cleveleys Avenue, and prizes were offered to architects and builders for houses and bungalows, some selling for as little as £200. Plots of building land of 600 square yards were on sale for as little as £30! And that was the start of Cleveleys as it is today. The population of Thornton Cleveleys was then 3,900 and there were 850 houses, nearly all in Thornton.

Before the 1906 exhibition, however, Mr Lumb became interested in local government and in 1901 he became a councillor for Bispham in the then Fylde Rural District Council. He was re-elected in 1903 when Bispham and Norbreck became a separate urban district. In 1918 Bispham and Norbreck Council amalgamated with Blackpool and in 1927 Mr Lumb became Mayor of Blackpool. He was enthusiastic in 1928 about the Blackpool Extension Bill, which sought to take over Thornton Cleveleys, but though that failed, Mr Lumb never wavered in his dream of a City of the Fylde. Oddly enough, despite his close connection with Blackpool, he never lived there, preferring to live in Thornton Cleveleys, where he occupied over a dozen different houses.

Soon after the end of the Second World War, he was elected a Freeman of Blackpool. During the whole of his council career he was a staunch independent. He never had any time for party politics in local government.

Mr Lumb designed the old West Drive Methodist church in 1905 and remained a trustee of the church. I first knew him when I started attending Sunday school there at the age of four, and he called me 'laddie'. I last saw him a few months before his death when he was getting off a tram at Cleveleys; despite his age he recognized me and called me 'laddie'.

Of his private life I don't know very much, but I do know how upset he was at the death in Japanese captivity during the Second World War of his grandson, a contemporary of mine. That boy's name was Tom Gallon Lumb, the same as his grandfather's.

2 June 1979

An ICI salt truck at the Salt Works.

Forty Years as Council Surveyor

The first few months of the twentieth century were notable in Thornton Cleveleys for the fact that the parish council obtained urban district status. This milestone marked the start of a forty-year career as Surveyor to the Council for Mr Henry Fenton. A detailed picture of the development of the district during that period is given here by Mr Fenton, who was also sanitary inspector, gas manager and fire brigade superintendent.

In deciding to apply for urban powers, the members of the parish council had come to the conclusion that the needs of the district, which was growing by reason of the establishment of the works of the United Alkali Company and the opening of the Blackpool and Fleetwood Tramroad, could be better met with wider powers in local hands. The urban district council came into existence in April 1900, being launched with the solitary asset of £15 6s 8d, cash from the parish council.

At this date the product of a 1d rate was about £60 for district rate purposes and as the district was committed to an expensive sewerage scheme, estimated to involve an addition to the rates of 2s 6d in the pound when completed, the prospect did not appear too rosy. The district may be considered up to this point to have passed through the 'incubation' period; it is difficult to visualize the conditions existing at that time. Highways needed attention – in the area of 3,000 acres over 12 miles of public highway were repairable by the inhabitants – and there was no provision for sewerage, removal of household refuse, or for the isolation or treatment of people with infectious diseases. There was an almost entire absence of footpaths alongside the highways (there were open dykes at the side of many) and no public lighting. There was one telegraph office for the whole district, no telephone facilities whatever, and no arrangements in case of fire. Against the asset of £15 6s 8d cash there was a liability of £27 4s 8d to the county council for their costs towards the public inquiry held before granting urban powers.

The urban council consisted of twelve members and although the original application for urban powers included a division into four wards, this was not granted owing to the difficulty in making a fair division of the electors. It is interesting to note that at the first ward election in 1904, seven out of the twelve retiring councillors failed to find a seat on the council, and among these seven there were four chairmen of standing committees.

After some inquiry and negotiation, Rossendale Bungalow on Victoria Road was taken on rental and a condition of the appointment of the first surveyor was that he should live on the premises, the council using two of the rooms. The present offices erected by the council in Fleetwood Road have been occupied since 1905.

Although one may term Cleveleys the 'shop window' of the district, the works of the United Alkali Company could be termed the 'backbone' because, though needing very little public service, they were contributing for a period one third of the total rate. The first venture into the realms of borrowing by the council was in 1901, when they purchased a steam road-roller for £430, which had to be repaid in ten years. The debt on this was, of course, extinguished long ago, and the road-roller proved to be a very good investment.

Bearing in mind that a 1d rate only produced £60 when the sewerage scheme was decided upon, that the cost to Thornton for its proportion was over £25,000, that the annual cost for interest, repayment and capital and the running of the air compressing station might involve an additional rate of 2s 6d in the pound failing a growth in rateable value, the importance of the scheme to the new urban council can be imagined. But happily, as one might anticipate, the inauguration of the scheme encouraged building and, although the burden was heavy in the early years, the increased product of the rate minimized the burden.

At the first election for seats on Thornton Urban District Council in 1900, the successful candidates were: James Fairclough, John Gleeson, Robert Hindle, William Carter, T.R. Strickland, J. Grimshaw, J. Titherington, W. Walsh, T. Rhodes, T. Walsh, T. Waring and James Taylor.

Amalgamation in various forms was in the air from the inception of the council. In 1911 representatives from Cleveleys were discussing with Blackpool Corporation the possibility of becoming part of their area, although Bispham was then a separate authority. In 1916, the proposed amalgamation of Lytham, St Annes and Bispham with Blackpool was assuming a definite shape and following the report of a sub-committee specially appointed to consider the matter, Thornton Council decided to inquire of Blackpool the terms and conditions on which they would be prepared to include Thornton in their extended area.

Owing to an intimation from the Ministry of Health that only agreed proposals would receive their support, the only amalgamation which then took place was that of Bispham, authorized in the Blackpool Improvement Act of 1917. Early in 1919, negotiations between Thornton and Blackpool were re-opened and finally terms were agreed upon and included in the Blackpool Improvement Bill of 1920. The opposition of the county council and the promise of a royal commission to consider the position of local governing bodies, particularly their absorption by other authorities, resulted in the amalgamation proposals failing to pass through Parliament.

It was unfortunate that no opposition was lodged by Thornton Council, because at that time the mains (gas) had not been extended through Carleton into Thornton and there was no immediate likelihood of its being done. There being no opposition, Poulton Council succeeded to all the powers of the company and it was only in 1905, when Thornton was considering the promotion of a Gas Act, that the mains were laid, thus establishing valuable goodwill. The Thornton Gas Act of 1906 authorized the council to construct works and to acquire from Poulton their interest in the Thornton district. The result of the arbitration between the two councils involved Thornton undertaking a capital expenditure of nearly £9,000 for which the assets capable of actual delivery could not have been worth more than £1,000. Fortunately, Parliament had allowed a period of thirty years for the repayment of the sum, but it was a serious burden for the new works to carry and emphasizes the necessity of a local authority guarding jealously against the establishment of monopolies in their area by outside authorities or other bodies.

Before proceeding with the erection of a gas works, negotiations were entered into with both Blackpool and Poulton for a supply in bulk, but as the terms offered would have necessitated excessive charges, the construction of the works was continued.

The foreshore and promenade at Cleveleys, the overlapping of the authorities controlling the surface water of the district and other maters of importance which it was found difficult to deal with without Parliamentary authority, gave rise to the preparation in 1911 of draft heads of a special Bill to be promoted in Parliament. A temporary improvement in one or two of the matters having been effected, and the costs of obtaining an Act appearing at the time somewhat prohibitive, the promotion was not pursued. The war and later the proposed amalgamation with Blackpool pushed any Bill further into the background, but when amalgamation failed in 1920 and as the council was not prepared to agree to new terms of amalgamation as proposed by Blackpool, it was decided in 1922 to promote a Bill which should provide for future developments as well as offering a remedy in matters which had been a source of worry since the formation of the council.

The main opposition came from the frontagers at Cleveleys, who objected to the payment of a special rate towards the annual interest on a promenade which was proposed along the seafront. Every endeavour was made to arrange terms amicably but without success, and the fight before the Parliamentary committee was a strenuous one, resulting in the principle of the special rate being approved although the proportions in the earlier years were eventually modified as the result of negotiations. The Bill eventually passed through the Upper House unopposed.

The costs of the Thornton Urban Council Act 1923, greatly increased by the opposition, were fortunately met out of balance in hand and the transfer of gas profits. The Act contains ninety-two sections, including the following principal provisions: (1) power to acquire the foreshore at Cleveleys; (2) construction of a promenade at Cleveleys; (3) power to acquire the

Thornton Bowls and Tennis Club, c. 1912.

river foreshore and the construction of a footway; (4) construction of a ferry landing opposite Wardleys; (5) road improvements; (6) special powers for ensuring the widening of roads when built upon; (7) transfer to the council of the powers of the Marsh Commissioners and Drainage Board; (8) construction of a new clough and the improvement of the existing clough for better dealing with surface water; (9) special powers for the regulation and better cleansing of watercourses; and (10) special powers for regulating the preparation of food and the manufacture and sale of ice cream.

The opening of the curve at Poulton in 1900 considerably improved the local train service; the opening of the goods sidings here in 1905 supplied a long-felt want; and the opening of Burn Naze Halt in 1922 has from the first more than proved its necessity.

The tramroad was opened in 1898 by the Blackpool and Fleetwood Tramroad Company (since 1920 owned by Blackpool Corporation) and inaugurated the development of the Cleveleys area. A test case between the Tramroad Company and Thornton Council was finally decided in 1909 by the House of Lords. The tramroad was held to be a railway and therefore only rateable (except for buildings) at one-quarter. This decision reduced the rate product for the district and created the need for a special rate of 1s in the pound to meet the balance of costs incurred after certain contributions had been made by Fleetwood and Bispham Councils, who were also affected by the result of the case.

The council fought a lone hand at the Quarter Sessions, in the Divisional Court and in the Court of Appeal, winning in the first two but losing in the third. They were then backed up by the two other councils, but only after delicate negotiations with the Local Government Board to obtain permission to join in the costs of another authority's case.

The power of Blackpool Corporation to run motor buses in any part of the urban district was obtained in the Act of 1920, this being one of the terms stipulated whether amalgamation took place or not. Blackpool was also bound under the same Act with the railway company to run a satisfactory bus service between Cleveleys and the railway station, and to construct mineral sidings at Cleveleys.

In their Bill of 1923, Thornton Council also sought power to run motor buses but in deference to the Parliamentary committee which considered the Bill in the House of Commons the clauses were eventually withdrawn as the committee did not favour the overlapping of two local authorities. After attempts at amalgamation had failed in 1920 the question remained in abeyance for a time, but in 1921 a petition signed by 78 per cent of the electors in Thornton Cleveleys was presented to the council praying them to re-open negotiations for amalgamation with Blackpool. Negotiations took place but the revised terms did not meet with the approval of Thornton Council and therefore the 1923 Bill was promoted to allow Thornton to deal with powers which would have been under Blackpool's jurisdiction had amalgamation occurred.

The provision of an efficient system of sewerage and waste disposal occupied the attention of the council from its inception. In fact, the decision to provide a sewerage scheme was arrived at by Thornton Council's predecessor, Fylde RDC. The original scheme – a joint one with two neighbouring authorities, Bispham and Carleton – comprised a tidal storage culvert in Anchorsholme Lane near Cleveleys Hydro and a line of cast-iron pipes discharging into the Irish Sea below dead low water. The scheme was arranged so that discharge from the storage culvert began at about half-ebb and ceased at about half-flood tide. This limited period of discharge was agreed upon after exhaustive inquiry into the direction and flow of the tides using an elaborate system of float tests which were conducted at the instigation of the Local Government Board.

In order to avoid the construction of deep sewers with flat gradients the district was divided into a series of drainage zones, in which underground ejectors were built in order to raise the sewage from a low to a high level. Extensions included the provision of ejectors, compressed-air mains and pumping or raising mains for the portion of Cleveleys known as the West Drive district and for the Stannah or East Thornton district in the direction of the River Wyre towards Skippool Bridge. These extensions, which were completed in 1926, also included the provision of an additional large ejector in the centre of Thornton, at Four Lane Ends.

In 1937 the council approached consulting engineers and a scheme was submitted to and approved by the Ministry of Health. Five new electrified pumping stations were constructed with a new outfall into the sea. A storage culvert was also built and the scheme was brought into operation at the end of 1938. The sewage was screened and only discharged on the ebb tide. The scheme cost around £100,000.

24 October 1953

ICI's power station at Burn Naze.

The Brightest Jewel

There have been occasions in ICI circles when the Burn Naze works have been referred to by local spokesmen as the brightest jewel in the Alkali Division's crown. No doubt Winnington Middlewich, Lostock and the other sparklers in the crown have something to say on that point, but as far as Thornton Cleveleys is concerned, Burn Naze has rarely been paid the tribute it deserves as the foundation stone upon which our modern town was built. Burn Naze, our north ward, is sometimes regarded as a Cinderella just because industry has eaten up so many of its green acres and the early builders were not inspired by the ideas that launched the Cleveleys Park estate.

The major part Burn Naze has played in the development of this district is underlined here in the story of the alkali industry's arrival by Mr James Sumner, who retired in 1943 after forty-three years working there. He is a Serving Brother of the Order of St John of Jerusalem and was responsible for the formation of both the Cleveleys and the ICI works brigades. As ambulance superintendent at the works from 1921 to 1944, he dealt with over 35,000 cases.

The salt works became industry's first intrusion upon the lonley acres here an soon afterwards came the alkali works. This was in the early 1890s. The salt works brought families from Cheshire – home of the salt industry – and with the alkali works' arrival, folk came from Runcorn, Widnes, St Helens, Northwich and Warrington. Houses went up by the hundred. Mr Heyes from Stacksteads, Bacup, built many of them and Sir Frederick Gamble, a director of the alkali works, gave his name to Gamble Road.

Let Mr Sumner take up the story of Burn Naze as he found it in his youth.

'There were no public houses, clubs or churches in the Burn Naze I first knew. The roads were so bad that men from the works took pieces of oily waste tied to sticks when they were going home in the dark. When burnt, these lighted the way. The nearest public houses were the old

Gardeners Arms and the Bay Horse. The Roman Catholic community went to Blackpool or Poulton for Mass. Until houses were built, the workmen had a special train to convey them to Fleetwood where they lodged.

Everybody in Burn Naze at that time was either farming, building houses or working at the 'Chemic'. There was a great building boom in the whole of the district from 1895 to 1915 and all the time the works kept expanding and there were about 1,500 men employed there. The highlight of the year was the Chemic Ball, a social event held at Fleetwood, which sometimes lasted from seven at night until six the next morning.

There were no doctors here before 1900 and the district was served by Dr Robinson of Fleetwood, Dr Williams who rode from Rossall on a bicycle and Dr Shikie from Poulton. Dr F.S. Rhodes, who became the district's first Medical Officer of Health, began his practice here aroun 1900 and for many years nearly everybody was attended by him.

As the smoke rose from the works' chimneys, the windmill, representing a much older industry, was still grinding corn and it was plain to see in the growing district that the value of Thornton was growing through the efforts of the Burn Naze people.

At one stage someone asked what would happen if the works closed and this caused the builders to look further afield. To the detriment of Burn Naze, there was a sudden movement to the coast and company houses at Cleveleys began to spring up.

About 1910, a public house was built at Burn Naze under the Earl Grey scheme whereby the thirsty were limited to two drinks – but this soon went by the board! Attached to this pub was a bowling green – the one still in use – and on it some of our best bowlers had their first lessons. Three who have been successful are G. Butterworth and J.H. Hill, winners of the Talbot, and W. Dalton, a Waterloo winner. Talking of sports, works teams have always taken a leading part in many activities and the transformation of the manager's house into the ICI Social Club and the building of one of the finest Scout halls in the country have been outstanding events.'

ICI's Hill House Works from the air.